Dancing with the Natives
A Philosophical Novel about Adolescence

Jeff Beedy, Ed.D and Matthew Cheney, Ph.D.

ISBN-10: 0-9855223-1-3
ISBN-13: 978-0-9855223-1-5

Global Children Publishing
235 N. Chesterville Road
Farmington, ME 04938-6223
globalchildrenpublishing.com

Contents

Foreword

Dancing with the Natives is a philosophical novel about adolescence. Metaphorically it describes how adolescents experience their lives and how adults come to respectfully dance with them. The period of adolescence is not unlike living on a remote island -- a place of isolation and separation from adults. No matter how well intentioned, adults are perceived as invaders. Like doctors arriving by airplane to a place that has never seen medicine or flying machines, trust needs to be earned through learning the natives' dance before goodwill is accepted. The same is true with the relationships between adults and adolescents. No power positioning or "I am the boss" posturing will take the place of unconditional love and time spent listening and respecting the rituals, feelings and thoughts of the adolescent.

One might say this book began with my own adolescence where, as an east-coast, long-haired cowboy, living in Maine, playing in a band while captaining a football and baseball team, I never quite fit in with any one group of my peers, and never seemed to understand the conventional -- I seemed to, for good and bad, to always do it my way.

These high school feelings about adolescence gained a theoretical life when I arrived at the Harvard School of Education in 1984, studying with adolescent philosophers Carol Gilligan, Lawrence Kohlberg and later teaching with Dr. Robert Coles. I was intrigued with Gilligan's notion of the adolescent as philosopher--a person with their own voice. During this time I also worked as a researcher at Mclean's Hospital on a four-year longitudinal study, listening for hundreds of hours to adolescents sharing their feelings about relationships with adults. The overall theme for these adolescents was the importance of relationships, and that adults simply didn't listen and understand. I could relate to their voices.

My theoretical framework for the book began at Harvard, but it has been my practical experience living with adolescents for the past 30 years that motivated me to write a book from the perspective of the adolescent. Over the past three decades I have listened to adolescents as I have driven school vans, lived in dormitories, coached baseball, skiing and golf and hosted hundreds of dinners at my house. I have paid close attention to which adults successfully relate to adolescents and which do not, which gain access into the adolescent's world and see it from the inside looking out and which remain forever pounding on the glass, left only to communicate with adolescents through muted murmurs and gesticulations.

In this book I want to share my humble view on how adolescents experience adults and why most adults have such difficulty establishing authentic relationships with adolescents. The book attempts to represent the adolescent as a philosopher, that is to say, as people with their own authentic view of life. My intent is to represent the period of adolescence as sui-generis, a culture of its own, with its own rituals and its own ways of seeing the world that are not necessarily as inchoate as we traditionally view them.

I view this book as a medium to promote discussion among parents, students, teachers, and communities. In this book adults cannot lead simply because they are the adults or because they own the power bestowed upon them as adults. There are dance lessons that adults must learn -- such as time, experience, and listening -- before they can lead.

I want also to be clear that I in no means feel I have mastered the dance with adolescents. What is actually closer to the truth is that I have learned more from my weaknesses and stepping on my partner's toes than I have from being a great dancer myself.

How To Read This Book

Dancing with the Natives began as a philosophical novel, but it became much more than that. For many reasons, the novel we began proved itself to be unfinishable. The journey of trying to create the novel, though, and much of the material that journey produced, fascinated us, perplexed us, challenged us. This, then, is a philosophical book about the failure of a philosophical novel.

We hope, though, that this is a useful book. We would like it to cause readers to think about their lives, because it has caused us to think about our lives, and we have both gained new perspectives because of it. This is a book for parents and teachers, for students and children. Each reader will, we hope, bring their own experiences and opinions to this material. We cannot offer any clear answers, but we can provide many questions that will, we hope, bring you toward answers of your own.

With that in mind, we recommend flipping through the book to see what is here. There is no need to start with the first page. Read around and see what holds your interest. Once you have a sense of what is here, you will know better how to proceed. If you want to start at the beginning, start there. If you want to go to the discussion questions at the end, go there. If you want to sort through the material in the scrapbook, you are welcome to.

There is no right way to read this book. There are wrong ways to read it, though -- it would be wrong to read it dutifully and without thinking, it would be wrong to accept all of the ideas without questioning them, it would be wrong to read it expecting simple solutions to complex problems.

If you are willing to read with an open mind, you will read this book well.

Jeffrey Pratt Beedy
Matt Cheney

Dedication

I dedicate this book to my dad, Dwight Pratt Beedy. He wasn't perfect but he could sure relate and I learned a lot of great lessons from him.

I have fond memories of my dad. He was a peaceful man who spent his life showing me that he loved me -- unconditionally. I think of my dad when I hear Dan Fogelberg's "Leader of the Band" verse: "His gentle means of sculpting souls took me years to understand."

There are so many examples. My father had a way about teaching me. He was not heavy-handed, but I knew what was important to him. To try to explain the depth of his spiritual power over me would be, I guess, a little trying to explain how David Copperfield actually pulls off his magic. In the end does it matter? What does matter are the memories he helped craft and how his influence has affected my life.

My Dad liked to garden. The fall spawned the harvest, the smells that developed my love for all vegetables -- even as an adolescent. Our garden happened to be located right next to the main road in our backyard. I was very athletic as a child. I was a pitcher and a quarterback for the football team. I liked to throw things. Anything. Baseballs. Wiffleballs. Tomatoes. One day in late fall a good friend of mine and I just couldn't resist the ripe tomatoes. We gathered up the biggest ones we could find and pitched the overripe tomatoes at the cars passing by. This particularly sunny late afternoon Mr. Bishop was driving by with his top down. I hit him square. My friend and I ran around to the front of the house only to find Mr. Bishop and my dad, talking.

I don't need to go into the details, but my dad responded to situation with both understanding and disappointment. What is important is that I too responded to the tomato-throwing incident with understanding and disappointment. I was sorry that I disappointed my dad. I was sorry that my tomato hit Mr. Bishop square and I never did it again. My dad did not use guilt or embarrassment -- he acknowledged the wrong didn't embarrass me stood up for me with Mr. Bishop and we all went away with a lesson learned. The point is I was as sorry and my dad never brought it up again. I learned a deeper lesson that lasted a lifetime.

As a parent and adult I am amazed at the absolute power that adults have on us as newly occupants of the second decade. It is true that we question just about everything. We are so unsure of ourselves, at least on the inside, on the outside we can be downright cruel. And, on the outside, parents and teachers aren't cool—they are fodder for jokes and "you are not going to believe what my mother said conversation." But we also love our parents. We watch them. We revere them and we know, at least understand that they brought us into the world. The lessons we learn, both good and bad, last a lifetime.

Mostly, I remember that my dad believed in me. This sounds simple, but when you are sixteen and desperately wanting to be a part of your peer group you need someone in power to believe in your dreams. In the summer of my sophomore year my parents were going through a rough divorce. My parents didn't have any money and there was a lot of fighting. That spring I had joined a local band. I asked my parents for an organ to play in the band. My mother said no and really did not give it much thought. At the time I didn't realize how little money we had as a family. But my dad knew what music, the band and the organ meant for me. Looking back now I am astonished to think that my dad with all his troubles spent time with me, listening to my heart and understanding what the organ meant to me. He went with me to the bank and signed for a loan—$600 dollars at the time was a lot. I made a commitment that I would pay the $60 monthly fee and I kept my promise. Besides the organ, which was important at the time, what I took away from the situation was my dad's belief in me and my dreams. The power that my dad used – understanding strengthened my commitment to keep my deal. Powerful.

CHAPTER ONE

You know you're in trouble when you've got everything you ever really wanted and yet your life still feels monotonous, like a black and white movie of somebody on coffee break.

I had a wife I loved and who loved me, adorable and amusing children, great and loyal friends, a job I'd always dreamed of having.

And yet...

The most challenging task for any of us, aside from getting the kids to take out the trash on Sunday mornings, is to give meaning to the everyday moments of our lives. It's about more than waking up and saying, "Boy, I'm glad to be alive." I can do that easily enough. The challenge is in accepting ourselves for who we are, and then taking that who we are and putting it into a community in a way that benefits both the individual self and all the various other individual selves that make up the community.

Lived well, life is a dance.

My problem, despite wife and kids and friends and great job (and dog — can't forget the dog!), was that I was galumphing, not dancing. I was walking like a goose with elephantiasis, stumbling and fumbling and somersaulting to no particular rhythm, with no grace, with no sense of where I needed to be or what move I should make next. A person can galumph for quite a while without getting hurt, but it's perilous. And it's ugly. I needed dancing lessons.

Not just any dancing lessons, but lessons in dancing in life. I would get these lessons on an island off the coast of a southern state, and my teachers would be more than twenty years younger than me — inexperienced in the ways of life, you might think if you glanced at them in a shopping mall or hanging out in front of a convenience store.

But I can assure you, these people — children, really — had developed more wisdom in their few years alive than I had stumbled on in all my years of galumphing blindly from one thing to the next. It took me a while to see their wisdom, and a bit longer to trust it, and even longer to really learn it for myself, but I can tell you one thing: once you've learned to dance, you'll never want to move in any other way.

***

I am the headmaster of a small boarding school in New England. Not the sort of school most people think of when they think of a New England boarding school — we don't have a dress code, teachers aren't all stuffy and erudite, and not too many of our students go off to Ivy League colleges. Ours is, for New England, a pretty diverse group of kids: they come from all over the United States and from about ten different countries. Somewhere around a third of the students are learning disabled (though we don't tend to use that term, since "disability" emphasizes the negative and we'd prefer to look at what students *can* do more than what they *can't*).

It's the only school I've ever been headmaster of. When I came, the school wasn't in very good shape. The previous administrations had made decisions which, at the time, had seemed necessary, but which, over the long run, had plunged the school into so much debt that we would have been forced to close the doors if we hadn't been lucky enough in my first year to find a particularly generous donor.

Not ideal conditions for somebody who's never been a headmaster before. We had to let a lot of faculty go, and we had to pretty much get rid of all admissions standards and accept any student who was willing to pay tuition. This meant that, for many students, we were a last resort.

Over the course of ten years, with the help of some excellent and creative colleagues, I had managed to bring the school out of debt, to strengthen admissions standards, and to rebuild the faculty until it was a group of people I was thrilled to be working with.

There was no reason for me to be depressed.

My wife was the first person to raise concern. She worked for quite a few years in public schools as a guidance counselor, and these days works for herself as a counselor specializing in adolescent psychology. (Since my own tendencies are adolescent as often as not, we're a good match.)

"You're a success, Ken," she said. "Success can sting as much as it can feel great."

"I'm not sure it stings," I said. "I'm just not feeling... successful."

"At what?"

"At education. Sure, we're financially solvent now, the bank's not going to come and close down the school, but what are we doing in the classrooms and on the fields and in the dorms? What are we actually *teaching*?"

"You've got a great group of teachers."

"Yes," I said, "but so do dozens of other schools. I look around though, and the kids don't seem excited to be here. I talk to them and ... hell, they might as well be in a minimum security prison as a school."

"That's kids," she said. "They're in the age when they don't like anything. Ten years from now, they'll be grateful. Look at how much alumni support you've got. They leave, and despite all their complaining, they have lots of fond memories, they think of this as a great place to have grown up."

I smiled and gave her a hug, but I wasn't convinced.

***

My closest friend on the faculty is an English teacher. In fact, he was my own high school English teacher — when I got the job as headmaster, I called him up and asked him what it would take for him to come work for me. He said all I needed to do was ask.

Jack Spencer looks like a stereotypical old school English teacher: he never goes to class without a tie and a coat that looks like he's been wearing it for thirty years (I expect he has). He smokes a pipe and keeps a copy of *Beowulf* in Old English in the bathroom for reading.

But there's a whole lot more to Jack than a stereotype. He flew helicopters in the Korean War and ended up with two purple hearts. During Vietnam, he marched with Martin Luther King and got arrested at anti-war rallies. He spends his summers volunteering at a Boston homeless shelter, teaching reading and writing. He has two Master's degrees, an old BMW motorcycle that looks brand new even though he rides it most of the year (until the snow gets too deep), and he collects vintage science fiction pulp magazines which, he says, he often reads late at night while listening to Schubert and drinking bourbon. He has never married, and I know nothing of anything resembling a love life.

Mr. Spencer's English class was a revelation for me as a wayward 17-year-old who was more interested in girls and rock and roll than reading. I'd probably never read a book in its entirety until I got to Jack's class.

I'll never forget the first day.

"Ladies and gentlemen," he said, sitting on the edge of his desk at the front of the musty classroom of a preppy boarding school I'd gotten into because my grandfather had been on the board of trustees, "I do not expect that you will *like* very much of what we read. We will be reading works that have, in general, excited and thrilled many of the greatest minds that have ever lived on this planet. Most of us are not great minds, and so we get bored with lots of pretty writing and philosophical speculation. This is natural. But just because something is natural does not mean we have to accept it. The one great accomplishment of this hideous species called human beings is that we have been able to extract ourselves from nature. We are not ruled by natural forces, although in the end we will be killed by them. Thus, my happy little creatures, we are engaged in unnatural acts in this class. We will read books you will not comprehend, and we will discuss them, and you will write essays about them. This is a crime, because good literature should be savored, it should provoke both thought and excitement. Since I cannot force you to be excited, I will force you to think. If you don't want to think, you're welcome to skip class and stick your head in a pile of horse manure, because the only thing that distinguishes you from a pile of horse manure is your ability to think, and if you give up that ability, then you are a disgrace to the already disgraceful history of humanity."

Jack then opened up an old, worn book of poetry and read some Byron to us:

So we'll go no more a-roving
So late into the night,
Though the heart be still as loving,
And the moon be still as bright.

For the sword outwears its sheath,
And the soul wears out the breast,
And the heart must pause to breathe,
And love itself have rest.

Though the night was made for loving,
And the day returns too soon,
Yet we'll go no more a-roving
By the light of the moon.

"That," Jack said, "is one of the most beautiful poems ever written. The music in it is, if your ear is tuned right, absolutely beautiful. What, though, is this poem about?"

Nobody wanted to answer.

"It's about sex, boys and girls. You know what sex is?"

We all looked away. Teachers don't talk about sex, or at least they didn't in those days.

"Byron's just made love to some fair maiden or another — or maybe a fair master, since he didn't discriminate — and he's telling her that though she might want more, more, more, he's got to rest a bit and he'll see her tomorrow night. The poem is on page two hundred and twelve of the anthology I have assigned you for this term, and I expect that you will read it tonight and come to class tomorrow with an essay of at least three pages which reflects on anything that interests you about this poem. Goodbye."

And then he sat behind his desk, lit his pipe, and continued reading the poem to himself while we all, a bit befuddled, a bit dazed, wandered out of the class.

Throughout the rest of the year, Jack spent a lot of time telling us what a waste human beings are, how we've squandered all of our potential in wars and massacres and stupidity, but that literature and art allowed us to look at the best of what humans were capable of, and we should worship it because of that, even when it frustrated us or made us feel stupid. "If you don't feel stupid in the presence of a genius like Shakespeare, then your ego is far too big for its own good," he said more than once.

With Jack leading us that year, we read more than I read for many college classes. From Shakespeare — *Hamlet, Macbeth, Twelfth Night,* and both parts of *Henry IV* — to *Gulliver's Travels* to Dickens's great school novel *Hard Times*, from *The Importance of Being Earnest* to George Bernard Shaw's *Man and Superman*; *Portrait of the Artist as a Young Man* to *1984* and even, in those days before feminism had taken much hold in private schools, Doris Lessing's *The Golden Notebook*, a book that completely perplexed me when it wasn't terrifying me. Jack's job was to give us a general survey of British literature from Shakespeare to modern times, and he did that. But he also gave us more: he gave us a way of looking at the world. I'll never forget him reading the World War One poems of Wilfred Owen and Siegfried Sassoon, tears welling up around eyes that we thought were made of granite.

Jack never slowed down if we got behind. He just kept going, and expected us to catch up. If we didn't, it was our loss. Few of us really kept up with all the reading (how could we?), but most of us paid far more attention to every word out of Jack's mouth than we did to anyone else at the school. And I know — because I have asked at reunions — that most of us have kept all of our books from that class, as well as all of our notes. And we've reread many of those books over and over again throughout our lives.

So when I sat down with Jack and told him about my feelings, my inability to feel like I was a success as a headmaster even though all of the outward signs said I was, I had one real question for him: "How can I make every teacher at this school like you?"

"Don't be a moron, Ken," he said. "If you had seventy of me, you'd go nuts. Everybody would go nuts. *I'd* go nuts."

"You inspire kids. You make them want to learn. That's what every teacher should do."

"I inspired *you*. I made *you* want to learn. What about the thousands of kids over the years who just thought I was a nutty old bastard who didn't give them a high enough grade?"

"They're the minority."

"I don't think so," he said.

"I know so."

"Well, I don't want to argue about it. What you want, what any head of any school wants, is for teachers to inspire students to learn, but there isn't one way to do that. You need passionate people, people who know their subject matter inside out and who live for that subject matter, and then you just need to give them space to make their own mistakes in their own ways. That's the only secret to teaching. It can't be packaged, it can't be quantified, it can't be commodified."

"It has to be," I said. "Good teaching is good teaching."

"Look, I spend most of my time lecturing. My voice is the one you usually hear in class. Go to any college and ask a professor of education what the worst technique for teaching is and they'll tell you lecturing. It doesn't work, they'll say. Well, it's all I do, and you think I'm pretty damn good. *But*, if somebody else, somebody who wasn't me, who didn't live to lecture, did it, it would flop. Just like if I started doing all sorts of stupid touchy-feely projects. It's not me, I can't teach that way. But I've seen teachers who are brilliantly successful that way, who never lecture."

"Okay," I said. "You're running a school. How do you structure it?"

He laughed and lit his pipe. "You don't want me to answer."

"Yes. Honestly."

He chewed on his pipe for a moment and then, more quietly than before, said, "The entire concept of school is a fraud. We lock kids up because we don't know what else to do with them. They're not really ready to be learning much of anything that they're learning, and most of it seems pointless and useless to them. If I were in charge of the world, I'd run it like Ancient Greece. Kids would go out in the world, they'd see what the world is like, they'd be working in apprenticeships, figuring out what interests them and also finding out that living is hard, making ends meet is hard, there's value in good work, all that Protestant work ethic hooey. And then I'd offer them the opportunity to go to schools whenever they chose. The schools would be there, open and free. No grades, just learning. Come and go at will. That's what my school would be."

I didn't know what to say, and Jack knew it. "I'm sure the board of trustees will love that idea," I said. "Parents and the state, too."

"I didn't say I was going to be practical," he said.

"No, you're right. Unfortunately, I have to be practical. And the practicalities are killing me."

***

I don't remember the exact moment when I decided to quit. There wasn't one single moment, really, just a lot of little moments. Talking with Jack solidified it. I agreed with him, and the more I agreed with him the more my job felt impossible. How would I ever be a success if my goals were idealistic? And yet how could I live with myself if my goals weren't idealistic?

The first person I told of my decision, or at least my desire, was my eldest daughter, Ruth. She was nineteen and had graduated from the school I was now thinking of abandoning. She'd been there through everything, seen the struggles to bring the school back to life, fought with me about various policies, even changed my mind a few times. Now she was a successful athlete and student at a good school a few hours away, and when she came home for spring break I sat down with her late one night and said, "I think I've done as much as I can in this job. What would you think of me if I started looking for another school?"

"I'd think ... I don't know," she said. "I've never considered the possibility. You and the school are one thing in my mind. Why do you want to leave?"

"Honestly, I'm not sure. I just don't feel ... useful anymore."

"What would make you feel useful?"

I chuckled. "Who knows. I keep hoping I'll know it when I experience it."

She gave me a hug. "Whatever you decide, I'll support you. But I'd hate to think of this place without you. Or you without it."

"Thanks," I said. "Somehow I've got to tell your mother."

"She'll start analyzing you."

"I know. Maybe I should have you tell her for me..."

"Don't be a wimp, dad!"

"I was joking. And loving daughters shouldn't call their fathers wimps."

"Yeah, well, sometimes you're a wimp. It's kind of endearing, actually."

I got up the courage to talk to my wife the next evening. It's not that I'm scared of my wife — I love her, she's incredibly thoughtful and empathetic — but Big Conversations inevitably turn into therapy sessions. It's a hazard of being married to a woman who spends her days helping people map the territory of their lives.

"Has this idea been with you for a long time, or is it just occurring to you?" she asked.

"It's been building up."

"How serious would you say it is? I mean, will you do anything you possibly can to get out of here, or can you wait a few years?"

"I could wait. I mean, I'm not unhappy, but ... I'm not happy, either."

"Josie's going to be a freshman in two years. It would be better to leave before then, or to stay through her time here."

"Right. Might not be much fun to be the headmaster's daughter."

"Ruth thrived on it."

"Ruth and Josie are completely different girls," I said.

"True."

"I guess I'm used to being able to do stuff people see as miraculous. Saving a school that's on the brink of collapsing. But now the hard work is beginning, and there aren't any miracles on the horizon."

"So do you want to spend your life saving schools?"

"Not a bad life," I said.

"And would you leave them once they're saved?"

"Do you think it's a cop-out?"

"I'm just trying to find out what you think. I don't really care one way or another. I want you to be happy. But if you're feeling like you're copping out and abandoning a place, I don't want that to happen."

"I don't either," I said. "But I don't know what I do want to happen."

"Well, don't make any quick decisions," she said with a yawn. "Time for bed."

I stayed up after she had gone to bed. I sat in our living room and looked out the big picture window which overlooks the campus. It was late, and the students were all in their dorms, studying or sleeping or ... well, I didn't want to think of too many possibilities. The view was a familiar one — I'd spent many nights looking out at the brick buildings, the long athletic fields, the big organic garden the head of the dining hall had started with a group of students who had complained that the food we served wasn't fresh enough. Lives got changed in those buildings, on those fields, and while pulling weeds out of the garden. Lives got changed for the better, mostly. What was nagging at me, then? What didn't feel right?

I looked up at the sky and the stars, the endless vast universe beyond us. It was a habit I'd developed after taking a class in Romantic poetry while I was an undergraduate English major. I started looking up at the sky at night and trying to see the wonders of nature, the tremendous magic of the nonhuman world. It put things into perspective. All those stars, all that sky, all that everything beyond us. How much do we really matter, compared to all that?

When we affect each other's lives, we matter a lot.

CHAPTER TWO

From the diary of Sonya Regensberg:

I've been thinking today about Nick when he was a child. After he was an infant, I didn't really want much to do with him — I was at college, didn't want the burden of a kid brother, wanted to make my own life, etc. He had been fun to have around when I was in high school, like a living doll my friends and I could dress up, though as I got more and more serious with more and more boyfriends, I certainly wanted to be away from home more. In college, though, I just didn't care, and I didn't pay much attention to the stories my parents would tell me about what he was doing, whatever trouble he'd gotten into.

I didn't really notice him much until that Thanksgiving after I'd begun work on my masters. He was nine, I think, and he refused to sit at the table for Thanksgiving dinner because he wanted to watch something on TV. My parents seemed fine with it, but I was horrified. It was Thanksgiving, it was us all together, a family, and here Nick was being a selfish brat. So I said I wasn't okay with it. If we were having a family meal, we should have a family meal. My parents tried to avoid it and say, "Oh, it's fine, really, it's just us, and we'll have a much better conversation if we let him do what he wants."

I should have known something was wrong then. I should have read the lines in my parents' faces better.

"Come to the table, Nicholas," I said, "we're having a family dinner and last time I checked you were part of this family."

He looked at me like I'd just dropped in from Mars. I told him again to join us.

"Or what?" he said. "What're you gonna do to me?"

"I want you to join us at the table."

"You're a bitch," he said.

I grabbed him by the arm and hauled him into the dining room. I wanted to slap him, I wanted to pound him into the floor, but, thankfully, I restrained myself. "Say anything like that to me ever again," I said, "and you'll get your mouth washed out with soap."

My parents shuffled and muttered, trying to defuse things, trying to pretend nothing was wrong. My mother offered Nicholas some dessert.

He broke from my grasp, grabbed a chair, and threw it across the room, smashing a mirror on the wall. Screaming a piercing scream, he ran out of the room to his bedroom and slammed the door shut. I heard things hitting the walls.

My mother stood quietly outside the door. "Nick," she said, "you don't have to do that, honey. Come have some pie. I made you your favorite pie."

My father tried to explain that this was what they'd wanted to prevent. Battles with Nick, he said, should be chosen carefully.

"You coddle him," I said. "If he's a brat, it's because you've allowed him to be one."

My father sighed and shook his head. I'm amazed at my brazenness, now, at my coming home for a few days and thinking I knew everything there was to know about raising a child. I hadn't had to sit through the hours of Nick's tantrums, hadn't had to meet with preschool teachers and kindergarten teachers and elementary school principals after Nick screamed at someone or broke another kid's toy or deliberately pissed in the hallway.

Later, after I had the breakdown and came home to live for six months, I got to know Nick. I learned how to love him, and I learned how terribly hard it was — it is — to love him.

CHAPTER THREE

Mornings are the best time of day for me. I usually wake up around five o'clock, I listen to music or read, I make breakfast for the family, help Josie get ready for school. The rest of the day is unpredictable — I'm seldom home for dinner, often don't even get in before Josie has gone to bed or Beth has settled down to watch the most brainless show she can find on T.V. to try to wash her mind free of all that she's heard, seen, and thought about during the day.

The morning after I resolved to quit my job, I sat in the living room of the house and listened (quietly) to a Neil Young LP. I'm old enough to still think vinyl sounds better than any sort of digitized music, and few pleasures are as pure and stimulating as listening to an old favorite on a turntable. As I listened, I kept thinking about my decision: What would happen? What would people think? What would become of me?

Josie and Beth woke, I made them omelettes and toast, and nobody said much of anything. We were sunk in the private worlds of our own minds, the worlds inaccessible to anyone else, the shelter of our inner voices.

As I was walking out the door that morning, Beth said to me, "Follow your heart." I smiled, gave her a kiss, and walked out into the chilly morning air.

My house is on the far side of the school campus, and so every morning I walk down the street and across one of the athletic fields to my office, which sits at the top of a two-hundred-year-old brick building without an elevator. The walk up the three flights of stairs is usually invigorating, but that morning it felt nearly interminable — each step seemed to radiate gravity.

As usual, my assistant, Helen, had gotten to the office before me. Helen is one of the world's great wonders. When I arrived, she was known as the headmaster's secretary, and she'd had the job for ten years. I quickly learned that she was far more than the term "secretary" implies, and I changed her title to Assistant to the Headmaster and added a $5,000 bonus to her salary. Though she isn't much more than five feet tall or a hundred pounds, she's fiercely intelligent, energetic, and indefatigable. Her Rolodex is the envy of the CIA, and if I didn't have her to organize all the various teachers, students, parents, and wandering salesmen who want to see me each day, I would end up quadruple scheduling myself and drowning in a sea of paperwork. She is also the only person in the school who knows how to make the coffee machine in the office produce something other than sludge, which has made her the most beloved person in the building, if not on the entire campus.

"You look weary, Ken," she said to me that morning. I have never known her to say hello to me, or even "good morning". Always, she lets me know if I'm looking alive and vigorous or slothful and downtrodden.

"Didn't sleep much last night," I said, forcing a smile.

"Why are you wearing a necktie? It looks like a noose."

"I felt like I should dress up today."

"People will think Beth dressed you."

"Maybe she should have..."

"I'll cancel that meeting with the Ziegler family. They can come tomorrow."

"With their lawyer." I had expelled Rusty Ziegler for attempting to blow up a biology teacher with a pipe bomb he had made and attached to the teacher's car. Luckily, Rusty had failed chemistry as well as biology, and his bomb did little more than puff out a few bits of smoke. Unfortunately for him, he'd also written a story in his English class about a boy who put a pipe bomb under a teacher's car, and his English teacher turned him in. He didn't deny doing it, but his parents thought the expulsion was a crime against humanity — after all, the bomb hadn't worked. Why not give him an in-school suspension for a few days? they asked.

"Mrs. Ziegler called yesterday," Helen said, "and she was getting all huffy, so I told her I'd be happy to have the chief of police call her and explain that making bombs is a felony. Suddenly, she was very quiet and polite."

I nodded, walked toward my office, and then stopped. "Helen," I said. "I was thinking ... I've been thinking ... perhaps..." The words seemed blunt and wrong to me.

"Yes...?"

"I've been thinking that maybe, soon, it will be ... it is ... time for me to move on..."

Helen cocked her head and seemed about to speak, but for the first time I could remember, she was at a loss for words.

Finally, after an unbearable silence, she said, "But ... *why*?"

"I think I've done everything I can do here. Somebody new, with new vision, a different sort of style, might be able to bring the school to a place that I can't bring it to."

"Why in God's name would we ever want to go to another place? The place you've brought us seems just right."

"Thanks. But don't you think a school is kind of like a shark? If it stops moving, it dies."

"A shark? Lord, no! For a guy with an English degree, you're not much good with analogies. A *shark*?! A school is not *like* anything, it's exactly what it is: a place for people to learn and grow and screw up and be cared for. That's what we've got. And we should keep it that way. You're an organizational disaster and one of the most frustratingly vague people I've ever worked for, but I wouldn't want to work for anybody else, so don't even think about it. I'll hunt you down and kill you, just like a shark would. Now go to work and stop thinking stupid thoughts."

I chuckled against my will, thanked her, and stepped into my office.

Someone once told me a person's office should be like stepping into that person's mind, but that most people's offices are like stepping into purgatory. I like to think my office represents my ideal mind — not only are three of the walls lined with books, but there's a nice view through big windows of the entire campus, and the primary decorations are vintage album covers: Bob Dylan's *Bringing It All Back Home*, Billie Holiday's *Lady in Satin*, Pink Floyd's *Murmur.* My desk is a small computer table. Two couches and a couple of chairs are in the center of the room, with a glass coffee table in the middle of them. Various piles of papers, magazines, and books are scattered on every surface, because even though the room is clean and almost orderly, I don't want it to give the impression that I'm less haphazard than I really am.

My general routine when I walk into the office is to sit on one of the couches, grab a magazine out of a pile, and glance through it for a few minutes before starting work. I subscribe to far too many magazines, and they accumulate in my office and house like dust or kudzu.

That morning I flopped onto the couch, knocked over a pile, and grabbed the first magazine my hand touched. It was a five-month-old issue of *Educator's Monthly*, a glorified newsletter someone had given me a gift subscription to for my birthday. I don't think I'd ever even looked at any of the issues before.

But on the fourth page, a headline caught my attention:

"KIDS CREATE EDUCATIONAL UTOPIA."

Utopia — literally, it means "nowhere". Because, by definition, a utopia can't exist. Perfection is a myth. The world is too complex and human beings are too unpredictable for any institution to be perfect.

But some young people on an island off the coast of a certain southern state say they have come as close to creating a utopia as anyone is ever likely to see.

They just call it "the island" and insist that the name shouldn't be capitalized. "We're not much into profound statements," said Cole Swenson, one of the young people I met when I visited the island for a few days in May.

It started when a group of kids from a wealthy suburb (they won't say exactly where) got fed up with school and decided to run away. It's a feeling many students have had — the desire to run away, to forge their own destiny, to be free of teachers and books and parents and curfews. These students, though, really did it. And not just for a night.

"When we got here," one of the founders, Rob Judenspiel, told me, "there was nothing. It was wild. I'd been reading Thoreau in school, and I'm an Eagle Scout, so I thought I was ready for the wild. But no. There's nothing like it. There's no way to describe it."

Wild. It's a word they revere.

"The island was wild, and so were we," Rob said. "We'd brought enough food for about a week. After that, we lived on some berries we found and all the fish we could catch, which wasn't a whole lot. But in less than a month we'd built the first building, we'd begun a garden, and we were surviving. Just barely, but we were surviving. Every now and then somebody would sneak back to the mainland to get some supplies — I don't think we could have made it otherwise — but it was always dangerous, because people knew us and were looking for us. We didn't want to be found. At least, not until we were ready."

By the end of the first six months on the island, the founders had built two sturdy buildings, created a massive garden, and begun formulating the most radical element of the whole radical project: a school.

Calling it a school is a bit of a stretch. "We were fleeing institutions," Rob said, "so we weren't about to create a new institution. But we knew we didn't want to just live on this little island for the rest of our lives. We wanted to use our experience to learn how we could become better citizens, how we could change the world. I know it sounds corny, but we were idealistic kids, and our idealism was the force that kept us working every day."

Over time, what was created could best be termed an *environment*. An environment of learning. An environment which encourages growth through questioning mixed with meditation and experience.

"The problem with schools," said Frida Welton, who has lived on the island for three years, "is that they aren't about learning. A school says: 'This is what you need to know. This is how you learn it. Do what we tell you and you'll be okay.' But who really learns anything that way? The people who have had an impact on the world have learned things because they felt a need to learn them. They learned them by struggling, failing, getting frustrated. They learned them by determining their own path. And that's what we do. We're constantly asking ourselves, 'What do we need to know? And how can we learn it? And then what do we do with our knowledge?'"

The people who live on the island — there are about thirty people living there now full-time, with plenty of visitors and guests — tend to be reluctant to talk about how their system works. Usually they deny there is any system at all. "We live together and learn together," Cole said. "That's all there is to it. It's the oldest recipe in the world for education: create a community, respect the individuals in the community, and what needs to be learned will be learned."

I was skeptical, sure there was more to it all, but in my short time on the island, nothing I saw indicated there was any sort of institutionalized system. I saw people talking, arguing, working together. I saw a remarkably well-stocked library. I saw people who, in another context, might look like juvenile deliquents working together to build tools, to cook meals, to sew and clean clothes, to renovate buildings.

And I never saw anyone over twenty-five years of age.

"We're setting out to prove *Lord of the Flies* wrong," Frida said. "And we're succeeding."

They certainly do seem to be succeeding. I contacted a number of people who had "graduated" from the island, and each had gone on to do impressive work. One had founded a soup kitchen in the heart of Philadelphia's ghettoes, one was running a health clinic in Kenya, one was the editor of a weekly "alternative" newspaper in Romania.

Why isn't the island better known? Why aren't their successes celebrated? Why haven't Rob and the other founders won the Nobel Peace Prize?

"We don't publicize," Rob said. "The people who need us find us. We do everything we can to keep everybody else away. We are lucky enough to have gotten a couple of philanthropists to help us, but pretty much we've done it all on our own. And we want to keep it that way. You're the first reporter we've ever allowed here."

And how did I get lucky enough to be able to go to the island? "We're pretty well read, and none of us had ever heard of the magazine you write for," Rob said. "That seemed like a good thing."

I doubt the editors of this journal would agree, but I'm eternally grateful. In a world of one educational failure after another, I got to be witness to a true success story.

I read the story three times, more excited with each reading. If my phone rang while I was reading, I didn't notice.

This was what I had been looking for.

This was what I needed.

This island, I thought, might be just enough to keep me from going insane.

I flipped to the front of the magazine and looked at the list of editors and contributors on the masthead. Listed as an "advisory editor" was Mark Golden, who had been on my dissertation committee. I hadn't talked to him for a while, but I still had his number programmed into my phone.

"Nice to hear your voice again, Ken."

"And yours. Listen, Mark, I need to get in touch with one of the writers of a story in *Educator's Monthly*. Do you know how I could do that?"

"Which writer?'

I glanced at the byline. "Sonya Regensberg."

"You're in luck. She did her Ph.D. here and I was her advisor. I'll have her call you."

"When?"

"What?"

"When will she call?"

"Is it an emergency?"

"In a way."

"All right, then," he said, "I'll do my best."

I said goodbye to Mark and then read the article one more time.

Helen knocked on the door and peeked her head in. "You have a nine o'clock meeting with the architect for the new dorm."

"Can you reschedule that? I'm expecting an important phone call."

"You had to reschedule him twice before."

"Then a third time shouldn't be a problem."

Helen scowled. "I'll tell him you're sick," she said.

Moments later, the phone rang. It was Sonya Regensberg. I tried to sound calm and professional.

"I'm curious about the island you wrote about in *Educator's Monthly*," I said. "I found the article extremely inspiring and I'd be curious to get in touch with some of the people there."

"Good luck," she said. "They're not very interested in having anything to do with outsiders."

"But you were able to go there."

"My little brother lives on the island."

"Oh," I said. "An inside contact."

"Some researchers have tried to visit, but the kids won't have anything to do with them."

"Why is that, do you think?"

"They don't like answering lots of questions from people who don't understand what they're doing. They think it's difficult for people to overcome their natural assumptions and prejudices and just watch and see what's going on. To observe without forming immediate conclusions."

"That seems reasonable. But I'd still like to try to get in touch with them, if I could."

"The best thing you could do would simply be to show up. They don't tend to answer letters or anything. But if you showed up, it would demonstrate to them that you're serious."

"Okay. Well. Ummmm. How do you get there?"

She gave me basic directions — go to a town down south, ask for Mickey at Mickey's Boat Shop, pay him $50 to ferry you to the island, and then walk a mile or so to the central square and ask to see a founder.

I hung up, then walked out to talk to Helen.

"Do you think you could clear my schedule for the next few days?" I asked her. "I need to go out of town."

She flipped through my appointment book. "You've got meetings with some of the faculty to discuss contracts. We can postpone those. And some parents … well, no-one I can't handle, I don't think. They won't like it, but I'll tell them you had urgent business. You do have urgent business, don't you?"

"Yes," I said with a smile.

"Other than that, I don't see any big obstacles. If people ask where you are, what should I tell them?"

"Tell them I'm off to … get some professional development."

She winked at me, probably assuming I was going barhopping with college friends.

"And see if you can get me a flight to Atlanta sometime tonight and a rental car."

"Sure thing," she said.
I began to walk down the stairs.
"Ken?" Helen called after me. I turned.
"Good luck," she said.

CHAPTER FOUR

From the diary of Sonya Regensberg:

I promised Mark I would write an article about the island, and now I'm wishing I were the kind of person who didn't feel obligated to keep promises.

What can I write? How can I possibly look objectively at it?

The kids on the island told me not to write anything specific about where it's located, who's there, etc. Am I bound to this? What are the ethics here? I want to write about so much — maybe I should write a book. But even a book wouldn't capture all the complexities.

Okay, let's brainstorm.

Did I think it was a model worth emulating?

Hmmm. Time for an easier question. What are the virtues of the island's culture/structure?

Freedom. This is a place devoted to freedom. What kind of freedom (remember Mark always harping on the differences between "freedom from" and "freedom to")? Freedom of choice: freedom to do whatever you feel moved to do. Freedom from coercion.

Except that's not entirely true. Everyone's first obligation is to the sustainability of the community, and once this sustainability is met, then they have the freedom to choose how they will spend their time. But if the food isn't grown or harvested, if the various products aren't made in the shops, if people don't have any clothes to wear, then there really isn't a lot of choice for anybody, because the place has got to be able to give food and shelter to everyone and it needs to sell stuff on the mainland to provide funds for the necessities they can't create themselves (granted, those are few). If the island had more needs and fewer people to meet them, it would have considerably less freedom, and we wouldn't find anything worthwhile in their lifestyle. The key is that they keep their needs few.

Lifestyle. Yes, that's an important word. I need to make clear in the article that this isn't an educational experiment at all, even though that's why I originally went there. People are educated, certainly — hell, lives are saved, and that's not a phrase I usually use with any confidence — but the education comes from the way they live. If you live there successfully, you have molded yourself (or been molded) to that way of living. Of course, that way of living is one that has a fair amount of leisure time, so people are able to be intellectual if they want, or they can choose to just vegetate or whatever. Kind of like how people have lived throughout human history — some use their brains and get enjoyment from that, some don't.

So what's the point of writing this article for an educational journal?

Education is one lens through which to look at what happens on the island. I've got to think of it that way. This is the lens I'm using, it won't see everything — it won't even see the majority — but focusing on one aspect may help us learn something important.

Right. If I repeat that enough, I'll believe it.

Not only do I wish I were the kind of person who didn't feel obligated to keep promises, but I wish I were not in education. I think if I were a plumber, I'd have a lot more to say about the island.

If I were a plumber, would I be so taken with the place?

Can't think about any of that now. I need to figure out how to write this damned article. Five hundred words, that's all they really need, maybe a thousand. Just some filler between the real articles.

Should I only talk about the virtues? Probably. Because I do think the virtues outweigh the flaws and the problems. I'm an ardent supporter of John Dewey and all the progressive educators who followed him (well, no, not all of them — refrain from hyperbole, please, Sonya), so I'd better think that the island offers more good than bad, because it's progressive education taken to its farthest limit.

Maybe that's a good working title: "Out on the Edge — Progressive Education in Practice and Praxis". (Got to throw in some good jargon like *praxis* — much easier to get tenure that way!)

Or should I write about the limits? Because that's the real value of the island's experiment: it shows us our limits. And boy are there some limits...

No. Too complex. Got to keep it simple. Just some basic information, an overview. If they want more, they can commission a book and pay me enough to take a year off from working to write the damned thing. (And that ain't gonna happen, so I'd better just be content with what I've got.)

The virtues. Yes, that's what it will be about. I'll try to keep it reportorial, because the farther away I stay from my own muddled ideas, the better.

All I really know is, I'm glad Nick found the place. It's no utopia, and it may be doomed and even destructive, but I know Nick would never have had the chance to discover himself as a real human being, rather than a collection of school expulsions and brushes with the local police, if he hadn't discovered the island.

CHAPTER FIVE

Mickey wasn't hard to find at Mickey's Boat Shop. He was standing at the back of a battered powerboat, hitting the motor with a wrench and swearing at it. He looked like a cross between a teddy bear and Godzilla.

"Excuse me," I said, somewhat sheepishly.

He continued to smash the motor with the wrench, shouting out a few words I hadn't even heard our students use.

"Excuse me." I said somewhat louder. "I'm looking for Mickey?"

"Yeah, that's me," he said, taking a moment to pause between swings.

"I was told I could hire you to ferry me across to the island."

"What island would that be?" he said, giving the motor a kick.

"I don't actually know the name. It's the one where some young people are living."

"Oh," he said. "You from a newspaper or something?"

"No," I said. "I'm a headmaster of a school up north. I'm just visiting."

After a final imprecation at the motor, he jumped down off of the boat and stood in front of me. "What do you want with the island?"

"Just to look. To ask some questions, see if I can learn anything."

"You're a little old for them," he said. "Not too many folks your age go over there."

"I know," I said. "But I think it's important."

"Well then," he said, "who am I to stop you? Fifty bucks, and I'll take you over half an hour from now."

"That would be great," I said.

Half an hour later we were riding across rough waters in a boat which I didn't think would be able to navigate a swimming pool. The heave and toss of the boat on the waves made my stomach lurch, and more than once I leaned over the side, ready to empty the chicken I'd had on the airplane into the sea. We had left at twilight, and by the time we got to the island, it was dark.

"Where do I go from here?" I asked as I climbed out onto the beach.

"Up through those trees, around a corner, then pretty much straight. There's a path. You'll see some lights. Just head toward them. You want me to come back for you sometime?"

"My flight leaves in two days, so I'll need to be back by then."

"I'll pick you up at eight a.m., how's that?"

"Great," I said, picking up the suitcase I'd hastily packed and brought with me. It was soaked and slimy from the journey.

"If you need to get back sooner, the kids have my number."

I handed him fifty dollars and walked into the woods.

There's no way to describe what I felt as the sound of Mickey's boat drifted into the distance and the rustle of the woods became the only sound I could hear. I've gone camping a few times, but I'm not really the outdoors type, and I had never before been wandering alone through dark, unfamiliar woods. I've spent most of my life in environments where I know the landscape, where surprises are few and control is ensured. What was I doing? I wondered. I'd woken that morning in my own bed, my own house, gone to work in my own office, and now I was ending the day in a world I didn't know, facing future hours I couldn't envision or predict. Was this responsible? Was it even mature? The decision to put myself here seemed at best impulsive, at worst idiotic.

It didn't take long, though, before I saw lights in the distance.

I wandered along what quickly became a well-tended path. It grew wider as I walked closer to the lights, until by the time I made out the shadow of a building in the distance the path had become the width of a road which two cars could drive down. The woods cleared and on either side of the road stretched large fields, perfect for playing soccer or even football.

The path ended at a crossroads, and directly in front of me stood an immense building of wood and stone, with large windows, six granite steps leading to the sorts of double doors you might usually expect to see on a castle, and Chinese lanterns hung along the eves, flickering in the soft breeze. To the side of the building, a few steps down the path to the right, I could make out some smaller buildings.

Past the big building, the path was lit with Chinese lanterns hanging from simple metal poles which seemed just about high enough to come up to my chest. The effect of the shimmering lights trailing off into a beveled darkness of shifting shadows was haunting — not frightening in any way, but rather the effect of a modest beauty inciting a primitive instinct of awe.

"Hello there."

It was a soft voice, and it came from a young man who stood in the shadows on the top step of the large building in front of me.

"Hello," I said. "I'm looking for one of the founders." My voice seemed high and wobbly.

"You're in luck. I'm Rob. I'm a founder."

"Wonderful! Great! Uhhh ... My name's Ken Murray. Mickey dropped me off." I hadn't planned out any sort of speech, any kind of explanation, anything to say at all, really. But I was here now, and I'd better explain myself.

"Mickey's a good man," Rob said.

"Yes," I said. "You're probably wondering why I'm here."

Rob nodded.

"I read an article about this — about here — the island — by Sonya Regensberg. I'm a headmaster, I run a school up north. I thought it was amazing, everything she wrote about, so I called her and asked how I could get in touch with people here, and she said the best thing to do, if I wanted to, you know, understand what's going on here, to really see, she said the best thing I could do would be to visit. To show up. And so, well, here I am."

Rob chuckled, then said, "Welcome. Do you want something to eat?"

"Sure. If it's not a problem."

"Not at all. Follow me, I'll take you to the dining hall and we can have a bit of a tour."

Rob walked down out of the shadows. He was older than his voice had revealed him to be — in his mid-twenties — with shaggy black hair and a thin beard. He was short and stocky like a wrestler.

We walked down the path beside the large building, past a series of four smaller buildings which Rob said were the shops where the islanders produced various items: baskets, paper, wooden chess sets, perfumes, soap, pottery, candles, and the lanterns used throughout the island for lighting — all prepared, primarily, from materials available on the island and sold on the mainland to help support the costs of various projects, mostly maintenance of the facilities.

"Are you completely self-sufficient?" I asked.

"No. We were in the beginning, for the most part, but now there are too many people coming and going for us to be able to rely on what we produce alone. But I'd say we're eighty-five percent self-sufficient. We try to keep our needs down, and if you do that, just stick to the fundamentals, you really don't need to rely on sources beyond your means. It's a good rule in general, actually, for any community: live on what you can create yourself. There's no better way to value what you've got. On the mainland, a farmer seems low-class, even embarrassing, easily stereotyped. Here, a person who can cultivate the land is a hero, because otherwise we'd starve. The knowledge that person possesses is revered, because it's the knowledge of life."

"At the school I work at," I said, "the director of food services helped the students create a garden, and now a lot of the food we eat, or at least the salads, comes from the garden. It's been a tremendous tool for their learning."

Rob nodded an assent, but he didn't seem as impressed as I'd expected he would be. After all, how many schools raise their own food?

Myself, I was quite impressed. Just in this short walk, I had learned much about the island, and from the little Rob had told me so far, I could guess about much more. This was a special place, I could tell already.

"That's the library," Rob said, pointing toward a rectangular building with long windows.

"What's it made of?" I asked, not able to see in the darkness the building's texture.

"A sort of adobe we developed by accident when we ran out of concrete and stones. Half-way through building it, we decided the library was too small, that we wanted room for people to be able to be comfortable, and we had dreams of getting enough books to make it able to compete with any university's library. So we built far more than we had gotten materials for. It's not the prettiest thing in the world to look at from the outside, but the wooden framing inside is wonderful, and we put in as many windows as we figured it could hold without collapsing. The floors are pretty thick. Books are heavy."

"How many books do you have?"

"Almost a hundred thousand."

"Good lord!" I said. "My school's library is seventy-five years old and only has thirty-five thousand books!"

"I guess it's all about priorities," Rob said. "What does your community value? We value knowledge, and the best source of knowledge, aside from wise people, is books. Therefore, we put a lot of resources into developing wise people, and we put a lot of resources into maintaining a library that goes beyond our immediate needs, because if you only look at immediate needs, then tomorrow you're going to suffer some painful surprises."

I felt that Rob's words were a sort of criticism, and I wanted to justify myself, wanted to say that I paid two librarians excellent salaries and gave them $40,000 each year for their budget, but I knew, somehow, saying this would be a mistake. I also knew that the budgets for many things other than the library were considerably larger than $40,000. Were these other things contributing to knowledge, to wisdom? I'd need more time to think about it.

I made a resolution, though: once I returned to school, I would work on finding a few donors to endow a larger library fund, and I would promise the librarians that I would double their budget within two years.

"Here we are," Rob said, leading me toward a building just behind the library, of a similar shape, but nearly twice its size.

"So you value eating as much as books?" I said, trying to sound witty.

"Can't read if you don't eat," Rob said. "But there's more to this building than just a dining hall. We've crammed in a bunch of stuff we didn't have room for elsewhere. The dining hall's the central part, but there's also an auditorium, some classrooms, lots of storage, and personal quarters. Actually, there are personal quarters in almost all the buildings."

"Personal quarters?"

"Dorm rooms, essentially. But we thought we needed a different name for them, because some people use them like dorm rooms, other people just use them for storage or for studying, or just getting away. Whatever they feel like. There are barracks in Founder Hall for people who don't want to sleep in their personal quarters, but everybody gets their own quarters, and privacy is strictly observed. There's not a lot of room to any of them, but it gives everyone a place they can call their own. So much is communal here that we discovered early on if people didn't have a place of their own, a way to get away from the community when needed, they'd just go nuts."

"And there are personal quarters in every building?"

"Pretty much. It started out that way from necessity, but now we plan it into any new designs or renovations. It seems to cut down on vandalism and that sort of thing, because at least one person has a sense of responsibility toward each of the buildings, since that's where they have their own space."

"Do you have much vandalism?"

"Here and there. Not much, no. But people are people, and most of our people are young, a lot of them come from difficult communities off the island, and so behavior is unpredictable, uncontrollable. People tend to take care of it, though. A sense of responsibility develops over time. If something needs to be addressed immediately, we bring it to the forum."

"The forum?"

"Occasional all-island meetings we have in Founder Hall. That's the big building where you found me. Come inside," Rob said, holding open a simple wooden door for me.

"Most everybody's asleep," Rob said, "so we should be quiet."

"You don't lock the building?"

"There are no locks here."

"Even the personal quarters?"

"We're not about keeping people out, Mr. Murray. We didn't have locks in the beginning, and we don't have them now. There's no such thing as stealing food here, since everyone is welcome to whatever food we've got wheneve r they want it, and if somebody wants to steal an object or item that is mine, well, there's probably a reason. But it hasn't really been a problem."

I began to wonder if I had stumbled on an island of unreconstructed Communists.

We walked into the dining hall. It was an impressive building — a central dining area with a cathedral ceiling filled with skylights, and stairs stretching off to the right and left toward a balcony circling the dining area, with doors leading off toward hallways and rooms.

"We don't have any meat, but I'd be happy to make you a sandwich or a salad."

"A sandwich would be great."

"Can you stand tofu?"

I gulped. I'd once had tofu at the school dining hall and found it to be like eating a soggy sponge.

"I'd rather not," I said.

"That's fine. I'm a particular specialist with tofu, but you can try one of my concoctions some other time."

We walked into a small kitchen area to the side of the dining room. Rob opened a walk-in freezer and pulled a few trays of vegetables and bread from it, then carried the trays over to a table in the center of the room, where he began cutting the bread and assembling a sandwich of lettuce, tomato, various beans, and cheese.

"It's goat milk cheese, but I don't think you'll mind too much."

"I'm up for an adventure," I said. Mostly, I was just hungry. "Are you all vegetarians?" I asked.

"Not strictly, but mostly, yes. It depends on how the crops are doing. There are times we have to supplement with fish, since they're easy enough to catch. But we try to eat animals only when it's a necessity."

"For moral reasons or health?"

"Both, actually. If we can survive without eating animals, then why should we cause suffering and pain to them? Meat is a luxury if you can live without it, and we don't want to kill animals for our own luxury. If there's no other option, and people are going to become malnourished, then it's no longer a luxury, and that's when we go fishing."

I wasn't sure I could live without steak or hamburgers, but I didn't feel mentally competent for a moral argument at that moment. I just wanted to eat the sandwich Rob was finishing.

"Try this," he said, handing me a plate with a sandwich overflowing with vegetables on it and a tumbler of water. The plate and tumbler were clearly handmade, the plate irregularly shaped like a galaxy or ink blot, glazed with a beautiful mix of deep red and black, the tumbler round and stout and glazed a dark green.

By the time we walked out into the dining room and sat down at one of the many wooden tables there, I had already taken three bites of the sandwich. I didn't know if it was my hunger or the food's quality, but I thought it tasted better than anything I'd ever eaten before.

"The bread is a mix of grains," Rob said. "It's an example of some of what we've imported from the mainland — we used to grow wheat and barley here, but decided that the amount of space it required was keeping us from growing other things we wanted, so we got rid of the grains and started buying them in bulk and bringing them over every month or so. It seemed like a worthwhile compromise, but we still argue about it every now and then."

"Do you argue about a lot of things?"

"We argue about everything. If something is worthwhile, it deserves being argued about. If people are invested in a place, if their lives are intimately connected to that place, then they're bound to have strong opinions about what happens there. Once people have spent some time here, they have opinions about everything. It's why turtles are often perceived as sort of arrogant when they get off-island, but it's also why they're so strong and successful."

"You raise turtles?" I asked, unsure if I'd misheard him or not.

"I'm sorry. Islands develop their own languages, and we're no different. A turtle is our term for someone who has been here for a while and who decides to return to the mainland."

"Ahh, yes," I said, taking another huge bite of the sandwich.

"Argument is not something we're afraid of. Conflict is not something we're afraid of. Creativity and conflict are linked, and progress almost always relies on conflict, on anger and frustration, on failure. We seek it. But we're careful not to be blind. The conflict which is bad is conflict where the participants are blind to their own capability for error. Error is nothing to be ashamed of, it's the key to moving forward, the key to learning anything. We aren't born wise, we rise from stupidity. From ignorance to knowledge. But it takes conflict to grind away a lot of that stupidity and make room for knowledge to replace ignorance. It doesn't matter how old you are, the process never stops unless you force it to, and if you force it to then you're blinding yourself and succumbing to the only shameful form of stupidity: willful ignorance."

My mind was spinning and buzzing as I tried to keep up with the ideas Rob had thrown at me, and I nearly choked on the sandwich. "You sound," I said, my mouth half-full of food, "like you've said all this a few times before."

Rob smiled. "It becomes a bit of a patter, I know. I've been here so long, I've worked with so many different people, that especially late at night after a full day of work, I fall back on words I've polished over the years. But please trust me: I believe everything I've said to you. It's not a sales pitch. I have nothing to sell."

"Except candles and lanterns and pottery?"

"We leave all that to the merchants on the mainland. We just provide the items themselves."

I had finished the sandwich and water and felt rejuvenated, but then the exhaustion I had been holding off with adrenaline began to sink into me.

"You look tired," Rob said. "Come, I'll take you to the personal quarters here and you can sleep."

We walked up a set of stairs, to the balcony, then down a long corridor, past numerous rooms of closed doors. Rob opened one of the doors toward the end of the corridor and silently gestured for me to enter.

He hadn't been joking when he said the personal quarters were small, if the room I entered was a representative example. It was barely large enough for me to stand in with both arms outstretched, and most of the floor space was taken up with a cot. Seeing the cot, though, made me desire nothing more than sleep, and I turned to Rob, whispered a thank you to him, and he closed the door behind me. I flopped down onto the cot without even taking my clothes off.

Shortly before I plunged into sleep, I thought: *In just an hour, I have learned more about education than I have learned over my entire career as a teacher and headmaster. What wonders here are left to be discovered?...*

CHAPTER SIX

From the diary of Sonya Regensberg:

Draft one completed. And it sucks.

First drafts always suck, I know that, but they also always feel like they shouldn't, like I've somehow failed because the first version I wrote wasn't perfect or brilliant. Brilliant writers are brilliant rewriters, I need to keep reminding myself of that.

I thought about faxing it to Mark to see what he thought, because I always value his criticism, even when it's harsh, but I don't feel like this draft is in the kind of shape that I'd want anybody else to read it. I also think I know what it's flaws are. What I don't know is how to fix them.

The flaws: too wishy-washy. Too many words. No clear point of view. My doubts keep filtering in here and there. The thing doesn't seem to know what it's purpose in life is.

The only way to fix it will be to lie. Well, not lie exactly, but whitewash even more than I originally intended. As I was finishing, I thought, "You know, if you just say it's a utopia and go from there, this will be a helluva lot easier."

I think that's what I'll do. Even though every cell in my body screams against it, I need to say the island is a utopia, and I need to allow its citizens to speak to that.

Besides, nobody expects a *real* utopia to be perfect. They just want it to be interesting. Wasn't that what we learned from all the 19th century experiments? Brook Farm, here I come....

I'm going to have to make up the quotes, because the few things I was able to write verbatim as I talked with people just aren't very helpful. I have various notes from different conversations, so I should be able to reconstruct them without too much inaccuracy, but it still feels odd. It's not like the kids are going to contradict me, though, so long as I make them look good.

Make them look good, yes. That's exactly what I'm going to do.

Because I've got to think about the larger implications. If I write this well, it could spark some interesting debate, it could get people thinking outside of their comfort zones, get them moving beyond the simple assumptions they cling to so ferociously. If I wrote it accurately, filling in all the complexities, offering both the things I love and the things I worry about, then it would be a much more accurate article, but it would probably be considerably less useful. What I need to do is present the island as a kind of model, and then let people pick it apart for themselves, because it's exactly that sort of dialogue which we need in education these days.

We need people to talk about why we make kids do what we make them do, why so many of our systems are coercive ones, and what gives us the right to make them so. I do think there are some very good answers to those questions, but the questions have got to be asked. If they aren't, if we just continue along on our assumption that the hoops we force kids to jump through are beneficial to them, then we risk harming not only millions and millions of people, but of creating harmful systems to be absorbed by our society. Imagine how amazing this country could be if we looked at our schools not as factories, but truly as places of learning — places to spark and excite learning, places to create *minds* and not just employees!

The culture of the island is one step toward that. It's not the only step, and it's probably not enough steps to walk with, but it's better than trying to stumble blindly toward enlightenment.

Yes, the kids are idealistic to want to change the world. But what's so wrong with a little idealism now and then? Shouldn't we be proud to have ideals?

CHAPTER SEVEN

Sunlight woke me. I lay in the small cot and listened to the bustle of people outside my room — a thrum of voices echoing up from the dining area, occasional footsteps in the hallway, the sound of people and machines outside.

I sat up and glanced out the window. My room was at a far corner of the building, and I could see the library in front of me and a few smaller buildings off to the side, in front of a long wooded area. In the distance stood Founder Hall, and past that some open fields bordering the ocean. People wandered through the paths between the buildings, always acknowledging each other, often stopping to talk briefly before moving on.

I took off my dirty traveling clothes and stuffed them into my bag after taking out new clothes for the day. Once I had changed, I opened the door of the personal quarters tentatively and looked out at the corridor to see if I could find a bathroom where I could freshen up before continuing my investigations on the island.

A young woman with short black hair braided in cornrows smiled at me as she walked down the hallway. "Good morning," she said.

"Uh ... hi," I said. "You don't know where there's a bathroom, do you?"

"There are composting toilets down on the first floor at the other side of the building. If you need to take a shower or wash up, you can do that at the bathhouse at the northwest corner of the pond. But that's at the other side of the island, so you should probably get breakfast first."

"Thanks," I said. "What's your name?"

"Marie," she said.

"I'm Ken. I'm a visitor."

"I know," she said, smiling, then walked down the corridor and disappeared.

I made my way down to the dining area and filled a plate with various fruits and a few slices of bread. For a moment, I was seized with an impulse to sit in a corner far away from anyone, to hide and pretend I didn't exist, for I felt conspicuous and alien here, so much older than anyone around me, so clearly lost, but I summoned up some last reserves of courage and forced myself to approach a table of people in the center of the room.

"Do you mind if I join you?" I asked.

"Not at all," said a boy with scruffy hair and big green eyes.

"My name's Ken. I'm a visitor."

They went around the table and said their names. I didn't remember them all, barely even paid attention to what they said, because I was focusing on their faces, their hands, their clothes. I was obsessed by a single thought: If there is hope for the future of the world, it is here, in these faces, hands, clothes. Bright, intelligent faces, the faces of people engaged with every moment of their lives. Strong, rough hands used to both manual labor and turning the pages of books. Clothes made by similar hands, woven with colorful threads in unique patterns, or simple clothes, plain and not ostentatious, the clothes of people who had better things to do than worry about fashion. But the ones who did worry about fashion — more boys than girls at the table I sat at, actually — what they wore was stunning in its simple beauty, its soft patterns of reds and blues and greens woven together like swirling galaxies or shattered cliffs.

"And you?" someone asked.

I pulled out of my meditation and said, "I'm the headmaster of a school up north. I've come to see what happens here on the island. People have told me it's a special place, and I'd like to learn about it."

"How long are you here?" a girl asked.

"Not too long. Today's my only full day."

"And what do you expect to learn?"

"I've learned so much already, just in the short tour Rob gave me last night. I don't know exactly what I'll learn, but I know I'm learning a lot. I'm learning what a community of people committed to learning values really looks like."

I smiled, expecting them to be pleased with my insights about their lives, my praise of their island, but though they smiled pleasantly at me, there was a certain wariness beneath their smiles, and their expressions seemed to be ones of amusement more than agreement.

"The island is a complicated place," the girl who had spoken to me said. "Keep your eyes open for..." Her voice trailed off.

"For what?" I asked.

She looked around the table, catching the eyes of the people sitting around us.

"For paradox," she said.

They had all mostly finished eating, and politely excused themselves, saying they had work to do and the morning was growing old.

I was alone. Hardly anyone remained in the dining area.

They were suspicious of me, I could tell. And why shouldn't they be? Here I was, twice their age at least, entering a world they had created, a community they were proud of. I knew I couldn't learn everything I needed to know about the island in a short amount of time, certainly not the amount of time I had allowed, but I was sure I could learn a great amount, and what I learned I could bring back to my school and use it to create, if not a replica of the island (impossible, I knew), at least a place which was a better community, a better school.

I finished eating my fruit and bread and returned the dishes to the dish room at the back of the dining area. Now it was time to explore.

Outside, the bright sun of the morning blinded me for a moment. I stood in the entry to the dining hall and waited for my eyes to adjust to the sun, then watched as people wandered past me, some of them carrying various items (backpacks, bolts of cloth, fruits and vegetables, hoes and shovels), none of them paying me any heed whatsoever.

What I really wanted to see was the library. I still couldn't believe that Rob had his figures right about the amount of books the islanders had access to. How would such a small group of people acquire such a library — how could they staff it, how could they organize it, and, most importantly, how could they possibly pay for it all?

I walked down the path and to the library. The front door was small, a simple wooden door on cheap hinges. I opened it and walked inside.

My first impression was that I was in a cathedral. Sunlight entered the massive library from thin, rectangular windows high up in the walls, casting sharp bars of light into the building, leaving much in hazy shadows.

The central room of the library seemed to occupy most of the building. Tall shelves of books filled the floor, and to either side rose long stairs reaching up to a balcony overlooking the main floor. The walls of the balcony were lined with bookshelves, all of them full.

Suddenly, 100,000 books seemed like a conservative estimate of the library's stock.

A few people wandered through the stacks, some others sat at long tables set around the perimeter of the room.

"I thought I might find you here." It was Rob. He had sneaked up behind me.

"This is amazing," I said. "I know university libraries that aren't this beautiful, this well stocked."

"We're very proud of it," he said.

"There must be a million dollars in books — more."

He chuckled. "Something like that, I expect."

"Were they donated?"

"A lot. We scavenge, too. You wouldn't believe what you can find in dumpsters behind bookstores and libraries. People are always trying to get rid of books they don't want, and we're known in the area as a place that will take any and all books. But we also buy a lot, since we like to keep current."

"The island's a more profitable enterprise than I would have thought, then."

"Teenagers are often thought to know nothing about money, but we've pretty well proved that wrong. I think teenagers are some of the craftiest businesspeople. They don't have enough adult biases about how money should be used."

Though I wouldn't have thought so before, intuitively I knew Rob was right. I made a mental note to investigate ways of having students join the development efforts at my school.

We wandered through the stacks. The books were organized well, and most were in good condition, though once I got close to them I saw that the collection was more motley than I had initially noticed. The scavenging was clear — lots of paperbacks with missing or torn covers and stained pages, battered hardcovers without dustjackets, thirty-year-old textbooks.

"Some of these — pardon me saying so — some of them seem like..."

"Junk?" Rob said.

"Yes."

"Many of them are. We've got a running debate going about whether we should cull the collection, get rid of the science books from before the days of slide rules, that sort of thing. Space is getting limited, so I'm sure we'll do that soon. But for now they aren't doing any harm, and they're interesting cultural artifacts. It's fun to see what people thought about the universe fifty years ago. A woman I've been mentoring did a fun project comparing various history books over the past few decades and how they represent different ethnic groups in their texts. Enlightening stuff, and not nearly as much change as you might expect."

We climbed the stairs to the balcony. As we wandered through the fiction section, I noticed shelves and shelves of science fiction novels and collections of short stories.

"Did some sci-fi fan send you a truck of old stuff?" I asked.

"Actually, a lot of us are science fiction readers. It's good for the imagination. And plenty of young people like science fiction. I think there's probably a correlation between people who are really intelligent but feel marginalized somehow and science fiction — it appeals to that sensibility. But it also helps foster a way of thinking that we encourage: thinking long-term, thinking beyond the present moment, thinking about possibilities and consequences of actions. To be honest, I don't really trust anybody who dismisses science fiction and fantasy. One of the problems of American culture is that not enough people are willing to open their minds to imaginative worlds."

"How is all this catalogued and shelved and everything? Do you assign people to library duty?"

"No. We don't have to. When we get new shipments of books, there are plenty of people who want to see what's there, want to add it all to the library. The work gets taken care of by people who are interested in it, and people who use the library all know the cataloguing system, so they tend to keep the shelves organized. One of the first thing we teach new residents is how to use the library. The catalogue is not computerized. We've talked about it, but we've got a very limited amount of electricity here, and since the card catalogue seems to be working well enough for everyone, there aren't any plans to add computers."

"You have computers elsewhere?"

"We have a few in the communication shed."

"Communication ... *shed?*"

"It's a little building. Some phones, computers, a fax machine, short-wave radio, that sort of thing. It's just across the path from here. The electricity comes from solar and wind, though there's a generator for back-up. We've only had to use it a few times. Consolidating where all the major electronic equipment is saves a lot of hassle."

We wandered down the stairs and out the front door of the library. "I want you to see Founder Hall," Rob said.

We walked down the path to the immense building in front of the library.

"This is where it all began," Rob said as we climbed the stairs. "The original was considerably smaller, just a rough little wooden building we built as quickly as we could so there would be shelter. It lasted a couple of years, but eventually fell in. By then, we had enough people and enough contacts to be able to start constructing the new building. It took almost three years of constant work."

He opened the front door, and I had the same feeling I'd had when I first walked into the dining hall and, even more so, the library: a sense of entering a vast, open space, a place the eyes and mind couldn't possibly comprehend all at once.

At first, the huge building seemed to be only one room. Large windows on all the walls allowed sunlight to fill every corner. Small wooden chairs filled the space and overstuffed cushions lined the walls. To the right I saw an open door, and inside the room a series of bunkbeds.

"Personal quarters?" I asked, gesturing to the door.

"Sort of. Barracks, really. For people who want to save their personal quarters for activities other than sleeping. It's hardly the most interesting thing here. Come on," he said, walking into the main hall.

"This is impressive," I said.

"We have all of our meetings here. Chairs for people who want them, cushions for people who prefer a bit more comfort."

"How do meetings work?"

"Whoever wants to speak stands in the center."

"Is there a protocol of any sort? Or is it just ... chaos?"

"Chaos is definitely a part of it. I guess there's sort of a protocol that's developed over the years. We're all too impatient, really, to be Quakers, so it's not like we just sit around and wait for people to say whatever they've got to say. There are different types of meetings, too — we only meet as a whole island every now and then. Mostly, it's just whoever is interested in what's being discussed. Somebody calls a meeting about something, puts up some posters, and whoever arrives discusses it. Anybody can call a whole island meeting, and we all show up, but you'd better have a really good reason, because if everybody shows up for a pointless or trivial meeting, you're likely to find yourself getting yelled at and then ignored for a few days, and the next meeting you call will probably only be attended by ... well, yourself."

"So people yell at each other? I can hardly imagine that here."

"It happens a lot, actually. People learn quickly to speak up for themselves, or they won't get heard, and sometimes to get heard you have to yell."

"I'm not sure I agree with you on that one," I said.

"Okay."

"Once somebody has to raise their voice, then it seems to me that they've lost at least a part of the argument."

"Sometimes, sure."

"And then what about the quieter people, the people new to the island? People yelling and all, I'd think that would be intimidating."

"It can be. But the thing is, you're looking at one behavior within an entire culture. What matters isn't the behavior so much as how the behavior functions within the culture."

"Give me an example," I said.

"If I were to go to a meeting at your school, and somebody said something really ridiculous, and I pointed out that it was ridiculous, but they continued along the same line of argument, not giving any real thought to my objection, then I would raise my objection again, probably more forcefully, and a lot of people would take offense, yes?"

"Possibly."

"Those people who took offense, would they tell me they were offended?"

"Sometimes."

"And if lots of people were offended — let's say I continued to press my point, and the person I was arguing with didn't acknowledge it and I kept pushing and we were getting nowhere. What would happen to me and the other person when we left that meeting? Would people still talk to us and pretend nothing had happened?"

"Probably."

"And quietly resent the whole incident, or talk to each other about what an obnoxious creep I am, right?"

"Something like that."

"It's not like that here. The person who hadn't acknowledged my point, who hadn't bothered to actually listen to what I had to say, would discover that his life got a lot more difficult, because people would be less willing to cooperate with him, to help him in the various things he needed help with. Not listening to people is one of the biggest crimes here. We have to rely on each other, to help each other out, and to do that we have to be able to trust that what we have to say, what we think and feel, will be listened to. Not agreed with, certainly not, but listened to. People who don't listen don't last long on the island. They leave after a few days.

"Now on the other hand, looking at how I had behaved at that meeting, I might have some problems, because anybody who thought I was obnoxious would not want to help me out with things, would probably not want to be around me except when they couldn't avoid it. And they'd tell me so. But if they agreed with me, if the person who didn't listen to me was particularly awful, had really ignored me, then I might get more sympathy, might even get some support and win some new friends. When I decided to press my point, I probably knew I was risking this, but the risk seemed worth it."

"You're talking about peer pressure," I said.

"Yes. But more than that. Community pressure. We have hardly any stated rules, but we have lots of rules that shift and change and are based on what the community feels, how the community as a whole reacts."

"That sounds a bit frightening to me," I said. "It seems it could be terribly oppressive, that tradition would be placed above individuality and people would be destroyed because they didn't conform."

"You're still not thinking about it in the context of the whole culture. It all depends on what the culture values. We have some simple values here, because we're a small community. First and foremost is the safety and health of the community as a whole — we've got to be able to function and continue, and we've got to be safe. If someone's individuality hurts the community's ability to get necessary work done, then we're doomed. But we value individual freedom almost as much as we value community health, because people have got to be free to pursue their own ideas and make their own mistakes. This, too, is a community value: we want to live creative, vital lives, and the only way to support creativity and vitality is to support as much personal freedom as can be allowed without sacrificing other people's health and safety. Even more than that, we try to encourage each other to find ways of living and working that are exciting and interesting. It matters to us."

I thought back to what the girl in the dining hall had said about paradox, and I began to think I knew what she was talking about. What Rob had said was so abstract that I couldn't completely grasp it, and what I did grasp didn't cohere, it seemed both impossible and eminently practical. I had a thousand questions, and I especially wondered how such a community and culture is created, because even though the ideas seemed amorphous and idealistic to me, they were also appealing. But I didn't have a chance to ask any of my questions, because Rob decided we should go for a walk to the beach.

"We've got two beaches," he said as we wandered back down the path toward the library and dining hall. "Long Beach and Green Beach. Long Beach is long and Green Beach ... well, it's not exactly green, but the water sometimes looks green and there're lots of trees and vegetation surrounding it. The swimming's better at Green Beach because the water's calmer on that side."

"I'm afraid I didn't bring a bathing suit," I said.

"Oh, we're not going swimming. I want to show you the Contemplation House."

"That sounds a little ominous."

"It's actually one of the nicest spots on the island."

We turned onto a path to the right just before we got to the library, and walked past a garden where a couple of people were planting seeds. A long greenhouse stood beside the path where it met two other paths. Beside the greenhouse was another garden, a large one.

"Is this where you grow all the food?" I asked.

"Much of it. The largest garden is on the other side of the dining hall. We try to rotate the crops a lot and replenish the soil as best we can. Some people have gotten very interested in horticulture and permaculture and a bunch of other things I don't really know much about."

"You mean there are things you don't know?" I asked. I didn't mean it to sound sarcastic or critical, but after I said it I realized there was a certain amount of frustration in my voice.

"I'm sorry if I've given you the impression that I've got an answer to everything. I don't. I've got a lot of questions, and plenty of them have to do with things I've talked with you about. In truth, I don't really know a lot, and certainly not as much as I'd like to know, but I've lived on this island for twelve years, and I helped create almost everything that's here, so I sometimes feel a bit protective of it, and I sometimes get so wrapped up in my thinking about it that I go on and on and sound like I know what I'm talking about."

"I think you do know what you're talking about," I said. "And don't forget there's a difference between wisdom and knowledge. I think you've got more wisdom than almost anyone I've ever met."

Rob laughed. "Oh god, don't say that. I'll feel like I have to grow my beard really long and spend hours stroking it and pondering the meaning of life."

We walked past a large building beside the dining hall, a building Rob said was "the Barn", where various livestock lived and equipment was stored. Past the barn were some small cabins, places for artists and craftspeople. As we walked, the path became more overgrown with vegetation, and soon we were in the midst of woods with tall trees and thick grass and bushes.

And then, surrounded by the woods, I saw a small stone hut. The Contemplation House.

Rob opened the wooden door of the house, and we stepped inside. It was a small, quaint place, with windows in each wall letting light slip in, making the room warm and comfortable. A few Asian rugs covered the stone floor, and comfortable-looking chairs stood near the back wall beside a fold-out cot. The house seemed to be equipped like a nineteenth-century peasant's hut, with a fireplace outfitted with iron cooking pots and a small wooden table nearby. One wall was lined with bookshelves, all filled with books.

"This is my favorite place on the island," Rob said. "We've created it as a place for people to get away when they need to. People can stay for as long as they want. Someone is in charge of bringing food and water once a day — there's some water in the bucket over by the door, and I've put some bread and crackers near it for you."

"So people just come here and..."

"Contemplate. Think. Use their brains. Meditate. Rest. Sometimes, you can't understand anything unless you get away. We should probably call it a hermitage."

"Fascinating. So you want me to stay here?"

"For the rest of your time on the island. You've seen what's worth seeing, so now we'd like you to remain here and think about it all. I'll call over to the mainland and have Mickey come pick you up when it's time for you to leave."

"But I'd like to talk to more people, to understand—"

"You won't understand anything until you think about it. You've seen a lot. You've heard a lot. Now rest."

Rob moved toward the door. I grabbed his arm. "Please—" I said.

"Mr. Murray, have you ever taken a dancing class?"

"Call me Ken, please."

"It takes a long time to learn the basic steps of a dance, Ken. It takes a lot of practice, a lot of looking like an idiot. It takes time. Well, what we're doing here is a kind of dance. And you need some time to practice a few steps."

Rob walked out the door and closed it behind me. I tried to open it, but it was locked.

"Hey!" I called. I was trapped. What could I do?

I tried to open the windows, but they, too, were locked. And even if I'd been able to open one, what could I have done? They were too small for me to climb through. And I doubted, this far into the woods, that anyone would hear me screaming.

I can't say I got much valuable contemplation done in the Contemplation House. I drank some of the water, ate the bread and crackers Rob had left for me, and pulled one of the chairs into the center of the room. It was even more comfortable than it looked — it was the sort of chair which, when you sit in it, seems to mold itself to your body. I mostly tried to think about ways to get free, ways to break through the stone walls or smash the windows and get myself the hell off this island, this place which had seemed so perfect and now had become a prison.

Eventually, after I'd passed through anger and frustration and restlessness, I let the silence of the house lull me to sleep.

I woke to the sound of the door opening. The room was darker than when I'd fallen asleep. It was twilight outside now, and the shadows of the world spread like long whispers across the landscape.

"Ready to go?" Rob said. He smiled at me.

"You little bastard. You locked me in here! You—"

"Mickey's waiting for you. Come."

We walked back to the center of the island, past the Barn and gardens, past the library and Founder Hall, then down the path I'd walked up when I first came to the island. At the end of it waited Mickey with his boat.

As I got onto the boat, Rob said, "If you feel the need to return after some time, Ken, please do. But we have one request."

"Yes?"

"Don't tell anyone about this place. Not yet."

"Why not?"

"Just don't, okay? We'll be watching."

Before I could reply, he had disappeared into the shadows.

The passage across the water was only slightly less dramatic than when I had first come to the island. But we made it back safely, and my car was waiting for me in Mickey's parking lot.

Before I got off the boat, Mickey took my arm. "He wasn't joking about what he said back there."

"Excuse me?" I said.

"Don't tell anybody about all this. For your own safety. Okay?"

"Are you — are you threatening me?"

"I'm warning you."

I walked to my car. It was dark now, and when I turned the headlights on, I could see Mickey in the distance. He held something in his hand. I told myself I was paranoid and exhausted, but what he held in his hand looked like a pistol.

CHAPTER EIGHT

From the diary of Sonya Regensberg:

Well, I thought the article was going to disappear without any sort of notice, but I got a call today from a headmaster at some prep school up north who was intrigued. Bizarre. That was just about the *last* type of person I thought would be interested.

I did my best to be helpful, but I was also worried about encouraging him too much — he really seemed to want to know what the island was like, and when I told him he'd have to visit for himself, he basically just said, "Okay."

Not that I think he'll do it. But I was flattered he'd take the time to track me down and give me a call. Apparently, he's an old friend of Mark's. I didn't know Mark had friends in the world of elite prep schools, but the man surprises me all the time. Next thing I know, I'll discover he's a cousin of the Rockefellers.

I'm surprised, actually, that the article hasn't gotten more attention. I guess I'd had my hopes up. I wanted it to be the start of a conversation. I wanted it to change the world.

No wonder I like the kids on the island so much. We're all hopeless idealists.

And then the horrible real world crushes us beneath its pragmatic boot.

Now I just need to move on. Forget the article, forget the island, trust that Nick is safe and happy, and go back to teaching classes, trying to get recalcitrant minds to open up and think about something now and then.

CHAPTER NINE

It was nearly dawn when I got home, and I felt like I'd been awake for a week straight. Beth was asleep when I climbed into bed; she awoke briefly, gave me a kiss, then fell back into dreams.

In the morning, I woke late, but after only a few hours of sleep. Beth had gotten up and made breakfast for Josie, who gave me a quick hug and kiss before dashing out the door to catch the schoolbus. I sat down at the little kitchen table and nibbled a grapefruit.

"So how was your trip?" Beth asked.

"Good, good," I said.

"What did you do?"

"Oh ... I saw..." But what could I say? Images of the island crashed through my mind, ideas and questions throttled each other, and more than anything else I remembered Rob's final warning to me, and Mickey's reiteration of it. And what he had held in his hand.

"I saw a lot of ... stuff."

"Sounds exciting," she said sarcastically.

"It was," I said. "In its own way. Unique, certainly."

"So were there a bunch of kids? Just running rampant? Or what?"

"No, no, it was tremendously organized. But, uh..." I glanced at my watch to try to avoid the conversation. "I've got to get to the office. Helen'll kill me."

Helen was thrilled to see me, and handed me a foot-high pile of papers and folders and memos to look through. She had scheduled a full day for me, and I felt obligated to meet with everyone I could and try to make up for my absence. But in many ways I was still absent; my thoughts drifted as people talked to me, and more than once I was asked, "Are you listening?"

Toward the end of the day, I called the dean, Tamara Kelly, and asked her to organize a full-school meeting first thing for the next morning. I wanted to tell everyone about what I'd discovered, and I wanted to begin to move the school in a new direction.

As I was finishing up going through some notes from the school's lawyer about suggested changes in the wording of our discipline handbook, and looking forward to heading home for dinner, talking with

Josie and Beth and Ruth, who had promised to come home to see me, Jack Spencer stepped into the office.

"Welcome back," he said.

"Thanks," I said.

"Actually, I've been looking forward to talking with you about it," I said. "I thought of you a lot. Kept wondering what you'd say to it all."

"It all?"

I then gave Jack a quick summary of my trip, trying my best to convey my sense of the excitement at the island, the creativity and cooperation which were so apparent. I carefully neglected to mention the last few moments, and Mickey's gun.

"Utopia's a dangerous concept," Jack said.

"This is as close to utopia as I've ever known about."

"The problem is that it's not sustainable. Any utopia has got to suppress change, because change would kill the perfection."

"What if change is built into the model?"

"Damned difficult," Jack said, stealing one of the pens from my desk and flipping it in his hand, a habit he had when he was thinking hard. "Change isn't something that can be predicted, and every utopia needs to be able to predict outcomes and effect, or else it won't be able to sustain itself. The nineteenth century was full of all sorts of attempts at utopias, and none of them lasted very long. The '60s had communes, and look at what became of them. Or the Free School movement. Some successes, sure, but ultimately failure."

"You're too much of a goddamn pessimist for your own good, Jack," I said. "You'd be amazed at what those kids have done."

I was surprised at how angry I'd gotten. Jack's skepticism frustrated me — I wanted him to be able to see how remarkable the island was, I wanted him to share my wonder at it all.

As we ate take-out pizza for dinner, I noticed that Beth was skeptical, too, though she didn't speak as bluntly as Jack had. I told her and the kids what I'd seen, using mostly the same phrases I'd used with Jack — "cooperation", "mutual aid", "everybody collaborating because of a sense of shared need" — and the best Beth gave me were a few grunts of amusement.

"Don't you think this is exciting?" I asked.

Beth raised her eyebrows, unsure what to say. Ruth spoke for her: "It seems to have really meant a lot to you, Dad. I don't think we really understand it all. I mean, it sounds, like, totally bizarre. A fantasy story."

"Yes," I said quietly. "I know."

"Can we go live there?" Josie asked. "I think it sounds cool."

Thank God for twelve-year-olds. But I needed a way to convince everybody of the magic I'd seen on the island, and get them to work with me to bring some of the magic, the excitement, the innovation to our school, which seemed to me to be at a perfect point in its history to learn some of the lessons of the island.

***

In the morning, the entire school assembled in the theatre, crowding the chairs and aisles, numerous people standing in the back of the room. The theatre was nearly twenty years old, and once it had been large enough to fit all of the students, faculty, and staff quite comfortably, but as the school had grown we'd spread to a size which only barely fit into the space, and the local fire chief called me at least three or four times a year to ask how we were dealing with code issues. ("Still thinking about them," I always said.)

I stepped to the front of the stage and spoke into a microphone which had been set up on a stand there. "Good morning," I said. "Thanks for coming in. I wanted to disrupt our schedule today because I've been thinking a lot about this community recently, about how we relate to each other, and about how we make decisions. I think it's time for some changes, and I'd like to initiate some of those changes today."

The audience was sleep deprived and not exactly attentive. People shuffled in their seats, leaned against the walls, yawned.

"I don't know how exactly to do what I want to do, but I think we're all smart, creative people, and I'm sure if we work together we can create some great solutions and come up with new ways to work with each other. This is our community, and we should take responsibility for it."

I paused, uncertain of how to say what I wanted to say. The silence crashed through my head and I spoke without thinking about my words. "What I want to do now is open up a forum for all of us to talk to each other. Anybody who wants to bring up any issue they have with life here is welcome to, and then we'll talk to each other and figure out ways to develop a solution. Please just speak up. Just say what's on your mind. Come to the microphone if you want."

Silence. Stillness.

I stepped away from the microphone and stood on the side of the stage. We waited. No-one moved.

Finally, a student with shaggy black hair and a weak attempt at a beard shuffled up to the microphone. He smiled, apparently proud of himself. "So why can't we have good food in the dining hall? I mean, how hard would it be to have Fritos at lunch?"

Lots of laughter. Some applause. The student walked off the stage, slapping a few friends' outstretched hands as he climbed back to his seat.

I went to the microphone. "Alright," I said. "What does everybody think? What would you like to see in the dining hall, and how can you make it happen?"

A few people shouted out ideas — more desserts, more soft drinks, a wet bar. Each suggestion got more and more absurd, until somebody suggested the school hire waiters who would bring caviar and champagne to every table at dinner.

"Okay okay okay," I said, raising my hands to quell the laughter and hollering. "Let's try to stay serious here. I'm trying to give you all some power over your community, and you're just saying all sorts of ridiculous things. If you don't like the food, what can you do to help make it better?"

The cacophony shattered into silence. "Doesn't anybody have any ideas?"

Somebody called out, "Why should we have to do anything? Isn't that what the kitchen people are for? Why pay them if you don't want them to work?"

"We eat the food," I said, noticing a sharpness coming into my voice. "It's our responsibility. If we don't accept that responsibility, we might as well all go home right now. Now who's got a productive idea about something?"

The silence of the room hit me like a storm, the hostility to my words raining down and soaking me. "If nobody's going to speak," I said, "then you have no right to complain about anything here."

A science teacher, a woman who had been working at the school for fifteen years and raised her family here, stood up and said, "Perhaps if we broke into small groups to brainstorm ideas—"

"No," I said. "We're a community. We ought to be able to speak to each other. We ought to be able to talk about the things which are important to us."

"But if we—"

"I don't want to hear from faculty. I want to know what the students are thinking."

She wilted down into her chair.

After a moment, a student stood up uncertainly and said, barely loud enough for anyone to hear, "Are we going to adjust the class schedule today? Are we cancelling first period?"

It was too much for me. I signalled to Tamara and walked off the stage, out of the building, and to my office, closing the door behind me and sitting at the desk, staring at a shelf of books I had never read.

Helen knocked softly on the door and stepped in. "Don't forget at noon you're meeting with the headmaster of the Riley Dunkirk School. I'll have lunch delivered."

"Right," I said.

"Sorry about this morning," Helen said. "It was a good try. Sometimes people just need time to adjust to new ideas."

"Sure."

"Want me to bring you some coffee?"

"No," I said. "I'll get it myself."

My phone rang a number of times, but I didn't pick it up, assuming it was either Tamara or some teachers who were offended that I'd told the faculty I didn't want to hear from them, a remark I would have trouble explaining.

Jack opened the door without knocking and paced from one end of the room to the other. "What was that all about, Ken? Huh? What kind of stupid, braindead philosophy are you reading these days?"

"Jack, I don't need—"

"It was embarrassing!"

"I know it was embar—"

"Did you *think* before you got up there? Did you have anything remotely resembling a thought in your head? Dammit, Ken, you're better than this, you're an insightful guy, you've got good instincts, but ... what was that all *about!*"

"I want to find ways to open this place up, to allow more people to make decisions about ... I don't know ... everything."

Jack put his hands on the desk and leaned over it, his face inches from mine. "We've got something good here, Ken. Don't screw it up by throwing it all away. Anarchy is chaos, and the last thing we need here is chaos. We've had enough of it in the past."

He turned around and walked out of the office, slamming the door behind him.

***

I went for a walk around campus before my noon meeting with Kendra Alexander, the headmaster (she loathed the term *headmistress*) of the Riley Dunkirk School, a school that was struggling with many of the problems my school had faced when I had first become headmaster. She'd called me for advice, and, since Riley Dunkirk was only an hour away, I suggested she come up and have lunch with me. I had intended to show her around, introduce her to people, point out the various programs which we'd implemented successfully, but after the disaster of the morning, I wasn't sure I knew anything about the school of which I was the boss, the captain, the figurehead.

I wandered past the old academic buildings, each of their dull red bricks whispering histories, and smiled at students who passed me, who all politely returned the smiles and said, "Hey, Mr. Murray," and "Welcome back," and "You coming to our football game tomorrow?" I hoped none of them would ask me about the morning meeting, hoped it had sunk deep into the haziest realms of their memory as if it had never happened at all.

I stood at the edge of one of the athletic fields and watched sprinklers shower water over the grass, sunlight cracking open in the mist. I fought back anger at our students, at the faculty, at Jack. They weren't to blame, even though their sense of entitlement, their love of their own privilege disgusted me. What would it take to make them see beyond their everyday reality, the routines they'd wrapped around themselves, the petty concerns and meaningless habits they called their responsibilities — why were all of the tremendous possibilities available to us invisible to them? Nothing was seared in stone, not the class schedule or the dorm rules or the meal times, not the grades or the game scores, not the rehearsal times for the jazz band or the hours the library was open or the length of faculty meetings. Everything was a choice, and we'd made the choices over the course of many years, but that didn't mean we couldn't make new choices. Indeed, wasn't it our obligation to examine and investigate everything we did, to see everything as flexible and impermanent? Wasn't it our responsibility to keep making choices?

Or would that only lead to the chaos Jack so feared?

A black dog wandered onto the field, dodging the sprinklers. It squatted in the middle of the field, took a shit, then kept walking.

That's exactly the attitude we need, I thought. Maybe the dog should be headmaster.

***

Kendra Alexander met me at my office, and we ate sandwiches Helen had made for us in the dining hall. Kendra was taller than me, had played basketball at Notre Dame, and wore a sharp blue suit and shoes with heels that looked like they should be registered as lethal weapons. "Tell me about your school," I said after we'd chatted a bit about our families and some of the gossip circulating through the private school network.

"We've got a quarter million dollars in outstanding debts, an attrition rate for both students and faculty that resembles a flood, a completely apathetic alumni base, and generally low morale," she said, the levity in her voice not quite enough to disguise the frustration and fear underlying her words. "And the board of trustees lied about most of it when they hired me. They alluded to it all, but it's considerably worse than anything they presented to me."

"But you want to stay?"

"I like a challenge."

I smiled, my first real smile of the day. "That's similar to what I faced when I got here," I said.

"And what did you do?"

"Triage, mostly. Tried to stop the bleeding. Put a few bandages on the old warhorse and tried to keep it moving forward. In some ways, it's a good position to be in, because anything you do that even mildly addresses the problems will be seen as a godsend. A lot of the decisions you need to make are already laid out for you, though not too many of them are very appetizing."

"Right," she said. "We've got to admit just about any student that's willing to pay, we've got to cut some scholarships, keep employee benefits to the minimum, address only the most immediate needs of the physical plant."

"And fundraise," I said.

"But it's hard to ask people to give money for a sinking ship."

"Which is why you need to come up with a vision that really inspires people. Set aside some money from somewhere and create all new admissions materials, get your alumni office to completely revamp everything they do, hire a couple people for development. It will cost you money you don't want to spend right now, but within a year or two it will pay for itself and get you out of trouble. But you've got to have a vision. That's what saved us. I was able to come in as a new headmaster and say, 'The school I want to work at looks like *this*,' and I'd give them some ideas, hand out a flashy new viewbook, and *bang*, somebody'd give me twenty-five grand to get going. Find twenty people who'll give you that kind of money, and all of a sudden you can begin building a new foundation. Five years later, you'll be out of the red and able to implement some good programs. Then you get to your ten year anniversary, and suddenly you'll find yourself having to make the truly difficult decisions, the ones that aren't obvious, where whatever you do it might be good, but you don't know what will be truly great."

"Vision, eh? But aren't people tired of being sold visions?"

"Some are," I said. "Which is why you can't have just any vision. You need to be able to tell people why your school is different from the other schools out there. It's one of the basic business tips: find your niche and exploit it."

"I know," she said. "I've tried. But I can't help feeling like, at the end of the day, we all do basically the same thing. And some of us don't have the resources to do it as well as the Exeters and Andovers of the world."

I laughed. "The minute you start thinking like that, you've failed. You're not in competition with those schools, and if you try to compete they'll kill you. You're in competition for the students who don't want to go to those schools, who couldn't ever get admitted to those schools. You're in competition with me."

"And you'll kill us, too."

"Not if you become the school for the kids who don't want to go to Exeter, Andover, or my school. And I think you're wrong about us all doing the same thing. I think we do totally different things."

"Such as?"

"The day I tell our students or faculty how to dress is the day I hope somebody forces me to retire."

"But that's superficial."

"Not at all. It's part of our culture, who we are. We want to be a school where people are free to make their own choices and decisions about how they present themselves. We don't want uniformity, either in dress or in thought. That spirit carries through everything that happens here."

"So you've got girls wandering around wearing minskirts and letting half their torso show?"

"Sometimes. Sure. Even in winter. But I also tell everyone that if they're offended by it, they should address it with the person who made the choice. If I show up in jeans, Helen always tells me I look like a car mechanic, not a headmaster. And that lets me get into a conversation with her about why I think it's good for a headmaster to wear jeans now and then, and why I don't think car mechanics should be degraded in favor of headmasters."

"See, I could never do that. Riley Dunkirk has always had a dress code."

"Which is fine. For you. It's part of what your school's about. But what's something you do that you haven't seen at other places?"

Kendra touched a finger to her cheek and thought for a moment. "Apple Day."

I raised my eyebrows.

"In the fall, we take a day off from school and everybody goes to a local apple orchard and picks apples. We bring them back to campus and bake pies for nursing homes and have apple-bobbing contests, that sort of thing."

"Perfect," I said. "Why do you do that?"

"Because we work hard and need to take a day off now and then."

"Which could be a central idea of your vision: work hard, play hard."

"We're not a sneaker company."

"But it's a start."

"Yes. A start."

"You've got to start somewhere, " I said, "and then just try to keep going without falling apart. Start from something simple like that and figure out what the implications of it are. What does it mean to work hard? And how can you play hard? How do you balance them? Start thinking like that, and you'll begin to change all sorts of things. You need a vision not just to sell to donors and potential students, but to use as a filter through which you see everything you do. If you don't have that, you'll just keep doing things because they make sense at the time, not because they make sense for what the school is trying to be."

She smiled, nodded, and took a big bite of her sandwich.

"It doesn't get easier, though," I said. "I mean, today I hate my job. I tried to change some stuff, and it was a failure. I don't know why yet, because I think the ideas were good ones, but they weren't ones people were ready for. So now I feel like the school isn't moving forward. And I don't know how to move it forward in a direction that excites me. I don't even know..." I hesitated. The thought had just occurred to me. "I don't even know if I believe in schooling anymore."

Kendra raised an eyebrow, perplexed. "You don't believe..."

I shrugged. "A momentary crisis of faith," I said. "Happens to everybody. Not serious at all. How's your sandwich?"

***

After dinner, Josie wanted me to play chess with her, but I hate chess and had a bunch of phone calls to make.

"You never play with me anymore, Dad," she said.

"Didn't I take you to that concert?"

"That was months ago."

"But you liked it."

"You're always busy."

"I've got a lot to do, honey."

"Can't you just play chess with me for half an hour?"

"Not tonight," I said.

"I won't get you in checkmate this time. I promise!"

"I said not tonight. Bother your mother."

I walked out of the house and to my office. I stayed in the office until eleven thirty, doing paperwork, replying to a bunch of phone messages which had piled up, writing a new fundraising appeal.

When I got home, Beth was waiting up for me, a glass of wine in hand.

"Josie cried herself to sleep tonight," she said.

"Oh? What happened?"

"She says she never sees you anymore."

"She sees me plenty."

"You should find time for her."

"I don't have time for anything, Beth. I need sixty hours in every day. I'm doing the best I can."

"You'll drive yourself into the ground."

"Maybe it's where I belong."

"Ken, what's going on? I thought your little trip to that island was supposed to reinvigorate you."

"It did."

"Well? What about us?"

"What about us?"

"Your family. When will you be reinvigorated about us, too?"

I sighed, then put on the best smile I could conjure. "I've never been uninvigorated about you, my dear. I'm just really busy."

"Don't let us disappear from your life."

"What are you talking about?"

"We shouldn't always come second to everything."

"You don't."

"That's what it feels like."

"It's late, Beth. I don't want to argue. I'm—"

"What?"

"I'm just ... tired."

Later, as I lay beside Beth in bed, moonlight drawing grey shadows through the room, I thought about Josie crying herself to sleep, and, though I hardly wanted to admit it to myself, I knew how she felt.

CHAPTER TEN

From the diary of Sonya Regensberg:

Got a letter from Nick today. He sounds like he's thinking about leaving the island. Part of me is thrilled — I really am curious what he'll do with himself in the world, who he'll become, because he's got so much potential. Another part of me is terrified, because I know that once he's back in the real world, having to deal with everyday, imperfect life, that he's just as likely to get himself shot or arrested as he is to suddenly blossom into the person I've long hoped he would become.

He said he feels like he's spinning his wheels. Yeah, well, welcome to life, kid.

But that seems to me to be one of the big dangers of the island — it's so small, so enclosed that there aren't a whole lot of options for people. They've got freedom, yes, but it's the freedom to wander around a few acres, to work in one of the shops or the gardens, to spend time in the library or the contemplation hut. Get tired of all that, and you can go play soccer if you can find enough people who want to join you.

It might have been enough for somebody five hundred years ago, but it certainly isn't enough to keep a mind that grew up in the complexities of the contemporary world from getting terribly, horribly bored. Human nature, it seems to me, is to seek out new challenges, and the island just doesn't offer enough challenges to keep the average person occupied for very long.

Which is part of its strength, as well as being a fatal weakness. It's the strength you get from a monastery or a rest home, the chance to relax and let your mind wander, to meditate and contemplate. Very important things. But then you've got to do something.

So I understand how he's feeling. I just fear that coming off the island will be such a culture shock that he won't be able to deal with it, that he'll fall back on old habits, or give up completely.

It all points out a strength of the kind of school system we have now — institutions that are part of the larger society, but which allow reflection on that society, preparation for it. Schools can be a safety net. Of course, if they offer too much of a safety net, then the net ends up strangling the people it was supposed to cushion. And if they're too divorced from real life, then it's like having a safety net underneath a high wire at a different circus than the one you're performing at.

One of the problems schools face, I think, is that they've lost contact with the world they're supposed to be a part of. They pretend, but their structure is so antiquated, their requirements and processes so useless to contemporary life, that they end up being a hindrance as much as a help. At the average school, the best thing to be is mediocre, because you don't draw too much attention to yourself, you get through everything without people bothering you. Thus, we have schools that teach people to aim for mediocrity, and then they go out into the world and do the same. What we need are schools that challenge their students to aim as high as possible in some direction and see what happens. They won't do that, because they want everybody to be at least moderately good at math and science and English and history and art and cooking and..... So they waste everybody's time.

On the other hand, too much specialization too early isn't any good for anyone, either. But we're the first society that's ever expected the majority of its citizens ages 0-18 (at the earliest) to be bland. Excellence requires an awful lot of time — I think I read somewhere that it takes 100,000 hours of practice to really become skilled at a difficult task — and so the people who truly become excellent in our society are the ones who find ways to make sure the school system makes as few demands on them as possible.

Seems awfully counter-productive to me. Unless, of course, that's the real goal: spread the majority of students so thin that they don't end up caring much about anything, don't end up being truly skilled at anything, and so are much more easily manipulated by politicians, advertising, hucksters, and charlatans.

Yikes — I didn't realize I was in such a cynical mood!

CHAPTER ELEVEN

Change would take time, that was what I had learned.

Change couldn't be forced on people who didn't understand where it was coming from. None of us are willing to change if we don't accept the underlying logic of the change.

I hadn't presented that logic to the school, I hadn't communicated my new vision, I hadn't told anyone about the real things I had learned on the island, because the things I had learned were still amorphous in my mind, and putting words to them was more of a challenge than I was prepared to handle.

I decided to delay any changes, save them for coming years. I would talk with people and communicate my ideas, I would try to get them to see things the way I had begun to see them, and with luck they would start to make changes of their own. That, I thought, was the real key to leadership: empowerment. Not forcing change on people, even if it seemed like beneficial change, but rather giving people the tools and authority to make changes in their own realms, changes that would filter up through the entire community.

The only big thing I did was double the budget of the library and instruct the librarians to use every penny by the end of the fiscal year.

A few days after my disastrous performance at the school meeting, the president of the student body, Reed Ingerman, sat down with me at lunch when we'd both gotten to the dining hall a little early, before the rush of hundreds of students and faculty filled the room with a teeming mass of hunger and noise. Reed was a star at the school, a talented basketball and baseball player as well as a strong student and devoted drummer who had formed his own percussion band and played throughout New England. He had the chiselled good looks of the stereotypical prep school kid, the kind of person who seems to have been bred to inherit great wealth and power, though in fact he didn't come from much money and was attending the school on a full scholarship, destined to be the first in his family to graduate from college.

"The comment at the school meeting about the kitchen staff bothered me," Reed said. "My mother's worked as a cook and a maid in hotels for most of her life. So people saying, you know, it's their job and not ours, it just really bothered me."

"Me, too," I said. "So what do we do about it? How do we change people's attitudes?"

"Well, there's already community service stuff that people do in the kitchen. But most of the contact people have with them is when they're doing work hours, getting punished. So everybody sees the kitchen as a place of punishment, the work as punishing. The food that we eat, we see that as somehow separate, as something that's provided to us, that we deserve because we pay tuition. It's part of the package."

"Right," I said. "And it is. So should we just admit this, or what?"

"See, the problem is that we don't see the people behind the jobs. The job isn't what's important — we've all got different jobs to do and we rely on each other. But who really knows the kitchen staff? I mean, who's having conversations with them about their lives? Most of the interaction is, like, 'This food sucks,' or, 'Bring out more hamburgers!' So none of us have any sort of relationship with them."

I contemplated the hamburger on my plate. "So we should find ways to change people's interactions with the kitchen workers?"

"Right," Reed said. "We need to know them the same way we know the teachers and dorm parents. The same way I know you. I mean, I feel totally comfortable sitting down with you here at lunch, and I think a lot of students do, and not just to complain about stuff, but to say, you know, 'Hey, Mr. Murray, how's life?' We should feel the same way with the kitchen staff. And the maintenance people, and the janitors."

"How do we do that?"

"Lots of ways. We could have a cooking class — Culinary Arts — and kids could work in the kitchen, learning the skills. Something other than punishment. They'd see it's a hard job, and that people take pride in what they do, even when it's cooking for four hundred people. We could even have a day when we cook for them. Faculty and students make their favorite recipes and the kitchen staff gets to eat and not cook and clean everything. Stuff like that."

"Good ideas," I said. "Get together with the student government, come up with ten ideas, check with the people involved on how to implement them, and then I'll make it happen."

"Cool. One more thing—"

"Yes?"

"How's life?"

I chuckled. "It could be worse," I said. "And you?"

"Same answer."

***

One night, I suggested to Josie that we go out for pizza together, a father-daughter date. She smiled the moment I suggested it and gave me a big hug. "Right now?" she said.

"Right now," I replied. "Get your coat."

We drove to the seediest little pizza place within fifty miles, a restaurant with faded magazine pictures of Elvis and AC/DC on the walls, its booths smeared with grease and grime which was, apparently, impervious to cleaning. A battered jukebox sat in one corner, and I gave Josie a handful of quarters to put in it; soon, tunes by Buddy Holly, Fats Domino, and Bill Haley filled the room.

"How's school these days?" I asked as we sipped big plastic glasses of Coke.

"Okay," she said. "I'm not best friends with Rena anymore."

"No?"

"She's so last year."

"Ah. So who's your best friend now?"

"I don't really like have *one* best friend, I've just got a lot of friends. We're like a gang."

"A gang?"

"Not like a *gang* gang. We don't, like, wear bandanas and listen to rap all the time. We just hang out."

"Uh huh. Well, don't go robbing any convenience stores or anything."

"*Dad.*"

"You're getting to the age when you've got to be careful about—"

"I know about sex, dad."

"Sex? Really?"

"We had to learn about it in health class. I put a condom on a banana."

"A condom on a banana?"

"Nobody else wanted to touch it, they thought it was gross, so I just took it from the teacher and put it on the banana. No big deal. And we talked a lot about menstruation. I know all about that."

"Well, I guess that's good."

"Puberty."

"Right."

"I think I'm just about to hit puberty. I mean, I've probably already *hit* it, but not like big time yet."

"Right. So what other things are you learning about? What are you reading?"

"I hate reading."

"You're killing me, Josie."

"I know I know I know — it's *good* for you and everything. But it's boring."

Our pizza arrived: half onion and mushroom for me, half Hawaiian for Josie. I lifted a slice from the tray and moved it toward my plate, grease dripping off it and splattering on the table like mucas. ("No grease, no glory," Ruth had said once when I'd been here with her and Beth.)

"So what are the boring books you're reading?" I asked.

"Just stupid shit," she said, then suddenly realized what she'd said and looked away.

"Glad you're learning some new words from your reading. What don't you like about the books? What makes them boring?"

"They're just about people who aren't interesting, they're not like me, you know, they have stupid lives and they fall in love all the time. Blecch."

"So you're not interested in people who aren't like you?"

"I'm not interested in reading about them."

"You used to love fairy tales."

"That was when I was a *kid*, Dad."

"So now what are you?"

"A young adult."

"Ahhh, yes, of course. I forgot. Shit."

We both laughed, and continued eating our pizza.

As we drove home, Josie said to me, "This was fun. We should do it more often."

"I intend to," I said.

"I'm going to be on the track team. Are you going to come to my meets?"

"Every one."

As we drove through the dark streets, the night felt formless around us, as if here inside the metal and glass of this little car, we were the only two people on Earth, the only two people alive, the only two people who mattered. It was a pleasant fantasy, comforting, and I discovered that I hadn't taken a short cut home, had instead decided to drive the long way around the outskirts of town, lengthening my time with my daughter, pulling us both beyond the realities and responsibilities of the universe outside us, as if our existence was on pause and the pause was a species of philosophy, one I'd long dreamt of but never known.

***

Within a few weeks of the end of the school year, I contacted Sonya Regensberg and asked her to come visit me at the school. I told her I wanted to compare our experiences on the island, and I wanted her opinion on some things I was doing with the school, changes I was thinking of implementing based on my experience at the island. I promised to pay all of her expenses and said I just needed to talk to someone with the same frame of reference that I had.

She arrived a few days later, and I met her at the airport, a heavy woman with short brown hair and piercing eyes, the sort of eyes that seem willing to see too much. We didn't talk much on the drive back to the school, though we did share stories about our lives, our college years and our current careers, the students we'd taught, the colleagues we knew in common.

I parked at my house and showed her to the guest room, let her unpack her bags and freshen up, then suggested we go on a tour.

"I've never really paid much attention to private schools," she said as we walked past a row of white, gabled houses which served as dorms.

"It can seem like a bizarre environment to somebody who's not familiar with it," I said. "We live together from September to May. We see students in the classroom, on the athletic fields, in plays, in the photography studio, and then we put them to bed at night in the dorms. We help them with their homework and then assign them more. We listen to their problems and share their successes. It's thrilling and exhausting, and I don't think I'd ever want to do another kind of job."

"It's not for everybody, though," she said.

"Not at all. Students or teachers. It takes a certain kind of kid who can flourish in this environment, just as it does a certain type of teacher. Somebody can be the best teacher in the world and still not be very good at this job, and most of them don't know it until they're here. Most of our new teachers stay for either a year or a decade, sometimes many decades. It's a way of life, it's not a job."

We walked through our two large gyms, past the fitness room filled with weight lifting equipment and exercise machines, and into the theatre. "We used to be a pretty jocky school," I said, "but the arts are my first love, so I redistributed the wealth, you might say, and now we've got equal money going to the arts as to athletics. Didn't make me popular with very many coaches, and I probably should have taken a bit more time with it all, but there was no way I was going to be head of a school that worshipped muscles and violence over brains and creativity."

"You shouldn't sell sports short," Sonya said. "They can be an amazing way to reach kids, especially kids you wouldn't reach otherwise."

"But the culture of sports in this country—"

"The culture is often a bad one, I agree. But it doesn't have to be. It's not the fault of sports themselves, it's the fault of the culture that has been built up around them. If what you worship is violence and brawn, what you'll get is a culture of violence and brawn. But sports aren't inherently about either."

We wandered on, walking into a building with classrooms, the computer lab, and a faculty lounge. I introduced her to a couple of teachers who were there, and then we walked to the library.

"The thing that impressed me most about the island," I said, "was the library. I just couldn't believe it. All those books. And for what purpose? It was just stunning."

"Yes, I wanted to stay and read for a week," Sonya said.

"I'm going to double the budget of our library here."

"You've got plenty of books already," Sonya said.

"It's all about that culture thing. What you value. And I think that, being a school, we should value books."

"Got to have people to read them," she said. "And time. That's the thing people often forget about books — if you're going to value them, you have to have the time to do so, and reading takes a lot of time. Having all those books on the island makes sense, because people have a considerable amount of free time. How much free time do your students have? How often are they just going to be prowling the stacks?"

"Well, they don't really have any free time," I said. "We schedule it all for them. Breakfast at 7, class at 7.45, lunch at noon, activities at 3, dinner at 5.30, study hall at 7.15, bed at 11."

"Then why do you want more books in your library? To look good? To feel good about yourself? Nobody has time to read them."

"I've tried to free up the kids' schedules, but there's so much to be done. What can be gotten rid of? Classes? Activities? Study hall? There are only so many hours in a day, unfortunately. We're a school, we've got certain things we have to do."

"And there's your biggest difference with the island. You're a school. They're not. Time is more relative there. They've got specific needs, things that have to be done, like making sure everybody has enough food, but once the essentials are taken care of, then they can do what they want. The essentials have to be attended to, but once that's done — and it's done quickly, because they cooperate on everything — then they make sure people are free to choose how to spend their time."

We left the library and began to walk back to my house, passing the garden the students had created with the director of the dining hall. "I'm really proud of this," I said. "Here's something the students work on with somebody they might not otherwise have contact with, and they get to see the immediate results, because they eat them."

"It's a good idea," Sonya said quietly. "Do the students decide to do it themselves, voluntarily, or is it part of another program?"

"They get community service hours for it. All students have to complete twenty hours of community service a year."

"Then it's hardly voluntary."

"They choose which projects they want to work on. Well, sometimes we assign them to projects, because each one has a limited number of spaces, and we try to balance it all out. Some of the projects are more fun than others. Seniors have the most choice, then juniors, and so on. Freshman usually get what nobody else wants to do."

"Which is completely unfair, don't you think?"

"Everybody has to pay their dues," I said. "We work our way up the totem pole."

"Spare me," she said. "Once people start talking about totem poles, I give them up for being hopelessly out of touch."

"But don't you think that a certain hierarchy is ... well, maybe not useful, but at least unavoidable?"

"Depends what you value," she said. "A system that has a certain group of people doing only the undesirable work while another group only does the desirable work is a system that is inherently unfair."

"But once you've done the undesirable work, then you get to do the desirable."

"The way you've set it up, though, is that you teach the younger kids that community service is something to be hated, something that they have to do out of some sort of undefined responsibility to something or other."

I was beginning to wish I hadn't invited Sonya to visit. No matter what I said, she had a criticism for it. If I looked at the school the way she did, I wouldn't see a success anywhere. And yet so much of what we did seemed to be working, so many of the programs that had been created in the past ten years had increased student involvement in areas that seemed important to me. Fewer students were skipping classes, fewer students were having to be expelled, fewer students were choosing not to return to the school each year. Faculty morale was up, our retention was rising, and we were attracting well-qualified new faculty. People were happy.

"You can't tell me," I said, "that as schools go we're doing a bad job."

"Not at all," she said. "But you seem to want to move the school toward being something other than what it is, something more closely aligned with the ideas that make the island so remarkable. If you're going to do that, you'd better question your assumptions. Just because something seems successful or interesting doesn't mean the philosophy that drives it is compatible with what you desire. If you're going to change people's lives, you've got to have a philosophical system you adhere to. The philosophy this school operates on may feel more progressive or experimental than that of other schools, but it's only superficially so. You're still subscribing to the basic philosophy of high school education in the United States, the idea that students are products and the school is an industry to manufacture those products."

"I don't think that's true," I said. "I've never thought of a student as a product."

"Not in so many words, perhaps. But look at all the systems you have in place: they're designed to shape students in a certain way, and then to evaluate how well the shaping has gone. Could you get rid of grades? No, because then you wouldn't be evaluating your product. Could you make everything optional? No, because then you wouldn't be able to predict outcomes and what the product will look like. Of course, you can't do that now, either, but at least you've got systems in place to make you feel good."

"So you think we should get rid of grades and requirements? Every school that's tried that has failed. Disastrously failed."

"Even if we assume that's true — which I don't — then what you've got to do is say, 'There is a thing called a school, and this thing has certain systems that are necessary to it being a school.' Until you come up with a different philosophy, the things that seem to be necessary to the idea of a school are things that view students as products and the school as an industry."

"Everything has to have a definition," I said.

"True. And the definition of an island is different from the definition of a school."

"Surely, though, some systems and ideas can transfer between the two."

"I doubt that anything could be transferred without somehow changing it. And what you've got to ask yourself is: Will the change that occurs during transfer harm the original idea?"

"And what do you think?"

She frowned and said in a tone that seemed filled with regret, "Since my article was published, I've had less and less hope for any meaningful transfer occurring."

We were silent on the rest of the walk to my house, and when we entered Sonya went to the guest room and I wandered into the kitchen. Beth was home, reading *The New Yorker* at the kitchen table.

"Ruth's coming for dinner," she said. "She doesn't have any classes tomorrow, so she thought she'd come up for a long weekend."

"Great. Sonya's here. She's putting her stuff away in the guest room."

"Did you give her a tour?"

"Something like that," I said. "She's already got my mind reeling. I feel like I don't know anything anymore. Whatever I say feels stupid."

"It's the natural effect of middle age. We get to a point where we realize everything we ever hoped to learn and accomplish we couldn't learn and accomplish in ten lifetimes, never mind one. It's why most idealists become conservatives later in life."

"Thank you, Dr. Murray," I said.

Beth winked at me. "Don't forget I charge by the hour." I kissed her on the forehead, then began rummaging through the cabinets in search of something to cook for dinner.

"So she had some good ideas? Or didn't like your ideas? What?"

"Both. I think she thinks I'm a nincompoop. I'm beginning to think so myself."

"What are you looking for?"

"I'm going to be a chef tonight," I said. "Try to redeem myself with Sonya."

"Or perhaps sentence yourself to eternal damnation," Beth said without looking up from her magazine.

***

I managed to cook us a surprisingly tasty dinner of spaghetti, complete with garlic bread and something resembling a salad. Sonya pretended to appreciate it all.

"You're a professor of education?" Beth asked her as we sat down to eat.

"Philosophy and education. I work at a small school, so I get to teach in a couple of different departments. My specialty is educational philosophy, so the college assumes that qualifies me to teach anything with the words 'philosophy' or 'education' in the course description. I've even taught a philosophy and literature course. One of my favorites, actually."

Ruth, who had driven the two hours home immediately after a softball game, heaped a gargantuan pile of spaghetti onto her plate and said, "I've been thinking of becoming a philosophy major."

Beth's eyebrows raised. "What? Why?"

"Because I took a really cool course last semester on Nietzsche and I think it'd be fun. I like ideas."

"What ever happened to becoming an athletic trainer?" I asked. At least she'd be able to get a job after college.

"It's boring. I mean, I like some of it, but I don't really care much about other people's injuries."

"Modern philosophy," Sonya said, "is a terrible field. Don't do it. Take a few courses, but don't let it be your major. Philosophy departments are full of people determined to prove that their abstract concept of the universe is better than somebody else's abstract concept of the universe."

"But don't you teach philosophy?" Ruth asked.

"Yes. But I teach philosophy as it's meant to be taught, not the way it's usually taught. Philosophy is about engaging with the world, putting ideas to everyday life, illuminating the experience of living. That's what it's been throughout most of history. Until the second half of the twentieth century, at least. Now it defines the worst connotations of the word 'academic'. Study science, study history, study anything other than philosophy, then go back to philosophy once you've got some knowledge. Nietzsche, after all, didn't do so well in academic philosophy himself."

Josie, half a strand of spaghetti dangling from her mouth, said, "When I go to college, I'm going to be a lawyer. They make lots of money. That way I can buy a big house."

I nearly collapsed into my dinner. "As you can see, we've taught her what's important in life," I said.

Sonya smiled.

"So you went to the same island that Ken did," Beth said. "What did you think?"

Josie nearly jumped out of her chair. "Can we go live there!"

"Maybe after you become a rich lawyer," I said.

After a moment of hesitation, Sonya said, "I think it's one of the most remarkable places I've ever seen. Perhaps the most remarkable. And frustrating."

"Why frustrating?" Beth asked. "Ken seemed pretty inspired."

"It's frustrating because it's inspiring. It makes you want to change the world. And then when you try to change the world, you realize ... well, the world isn't exactly clamoring for change. In fact, the world's pretty well set up to avoid change, to fear it and destroy it."

"But small changes are possible," Ruth said. "And enough small changes can add up. I mean, I've been working with an environmental club at school, and we've got the whole school recycling now, and we've almost got the administration to agree to buy only recycled paper for the copy machines. Each year, we make progress."

"But the sort of changes the island makes you yearn for," I said, "require thousands, maybe millions, of small changes. Hundreds of years of small changes."

"Got to start somewhere," Ruth said.

"That's like I've decided to stop calling Warner a stupid fatso every time I see him," Josie said. "He says I'm a snotty little brat, and so I decided if I stop calling him a stupid fatso, maybe he'll stop calling me a stupid little brat. I think we're too old to keep doing that."

We all laughed, and Josie seemed taken aback. "It was mom's idea," she whispered.

"Ruth's right," I said. "We've got to start somewhere. So, Sonya, I've arranged a meeting tomorrow with a couple of students and some faculty I think you should meet. There's no agenda, I'd just like you to ... well, to be honest, I'd like you to question their assumptions."

"It's one of my favorite activities," she said.

***

We held the meeting in a corner of the library where we could all sit in comfortable, overstuffed armchairs. I had invited Jack Spencer, Reed Ingerman, and Tamara Kelly as well as a new math teacher, Julie Gardiner, who had shown a lot of interest in making math a more palatable subject for students who otherwise hated it; Ross Ziegler, who taught biology and ecology and had been the first person to suggest creating the garden the students worked on for community service; Gerry Krupinski, the head of the dining hall; and the presidents of each of the classes: Sandy Mangold, Will Sargoff, Allen Hirst, and Jen Torvald.

"I asked you all to meet with me today," I said, "because I want to get some ideas floating around here. You all know I've been away, but I haven't told you much about why I was gone or where I went. I think now is the time to let you know."

I did my best to summarize my experience on the island for them, mostly just trying to describe what I had seen and some of the things Rob had said to me. Then I introduced Sonya.

"I've asked Sonya to talk to us both because she's had first-hand experience of the island, and because she's quite skilled at looking closely at ideas we might take for granted."

Jack had been sitting impatiently through my whole introduction, and now he said, "So are you suggesting that you think this school should become more like this utopian island you say you visited?"

"I don't think we would suffer much if we were to be like the island," I said, "but I also recognize that we've got our own struggles and challenges, and that, as Sonya has so forcefully pointed out to me, a school is not an island. However, I think that we can use some of the lessons of the island to improve what we do here."

Jack scowled and sat back in his chair, but said nothing.

Sonya said, "I'm a little less idealistic than Ken. I think the ways of the islanders can teach us a lot about how to relate to one another in society, but I'm not sure they can teach us much about school."

"Isn't school a part of society?" Reed asked.

"Yes, but it's an institution in the society. Institutions tend to be difficult to change; often, they can only be destroyed and built anew."

"I disagree," Julie said. "The history of the U.S. is the history of institutions being reformed. Look at where we've gotten since 1775."

"A perfect example," Sonya said. "More than two hundred years of reform. Incremental reform. Wars, labor struggles, civil rights movements. Tension and conflict. That's where the reform has come from. The institutions being threatened with death over and over again. Compromise. Endless compromise. So, yes, there've been plenty of reforms since 1775, but none of them have been particularly revolutionary, and few of them happened quickly."

"What if small reforms are all that an institution needs?" Will asked.

"Then there's not likely to be a big problem. Which is exactly why I'd ask Ken here one question: What is so wrong with how your school does things? Why are you so interested in sudden changes?"

"Because I've seen what is possible," I said.

"He's had a dream!" Jack shouted, his voice echoing through the entire building.

Sonya said, "Why does what you saw make you want to change things here? Why is what you do here not acceptable?"

It was the sort of question I wished I had a day, or even a year, to answer, because whatever I said now was likely to be either wrong or, at best, superficial. The truth was that the way we were functioning at the school *felt* wrong to me, but I didn't have the words to express the feeling, because I had not yet attached words to the feeling. "I want to be at a school," I said, "where freedom and creativity are combined to help everyone become better thinkers and better citizens."

Even I thought I sounded like a used car salesman.

Sonya took me seriously, though. "That's a noble goal. High falutin', but noble." She turned to the others. "What keeps this school from maximizing freedom and creativity?"

"Rules," said Sandy.

Tamara chuckled. Sonya scowled at her. "It's a perfectly legitimate answer. Rules impinge on freedom. Is it necessary to have rules?"

"Of course," Tamara said. "Otherwise nobody would do anything. Or they'd do whatever they felt like."

"And what do they feel like doing?"

"Not going to classes. Smoking, drinking, having sex." She turned to the students. "Right?"

The students smiled, but Sonya jumped in immediately. "Given total freedom with your life, what would you do?"

Allen said, "What I'd do is different from what other people would do. Sure, plenty of kids would want to do, you know, everything Mrs. Kelly said, but not everybody. It's not like we don't already have the opportunity to do that stuff. I'd still go to school, because I want to go to a good college so I can get a good job and support a family. I'd go to the classes I liked."

"But not all the classes you need are ones you like," Ross said.

Jen said, "If the college you want to go to says you need three years of a foreign language, then aren't you going to take three years of a foreign language, even if you don't like it?"

"How many of us think that far ahead?" Reed asked. He turned to Sandy. "You're a freshman. Are you thinking now about what classes you'll need to take here so you can get into college?"

"Sometimes," Sandy said. "Not much, though. They tell us what we need, so we don't have to think about it."

"So what would happen," I said, "if at the beginning of the year everybody worked with their advisor to set some goals, goals for the year and goals for the next few years, maybe even goals for ten years from now, and then looked at what was available here and chose the things they did based on those goals? Would we still need any sorts of requirements?"

"We'd still need rules," Tamara said.

"Which rules?" Sonya asked.

"No drugs, no beating people up, no sex. The basic rules."

"Why?" Sonya asked.

"*Why?!* Are you nuts?"

Sonya smiled and said, "We're doing a thought experiment. Work with me. Why do you need those rules?"

"Because parents expect them. Nobody's going to send their kid to a school that lets students do pot and get laid all the time."

"Why?"

"You sound just like my two-year-old," Tamara said. "Why why why! Because it's unsafe, it's illegal, it's—"

"Exactly. And the school as an institution has an abiding concern in protecting students' safety and making sure no laws are broken."

"Yes."

"Seems reasonable to me," Sonya said. "Would anyone vote to get rid of reasonable rules, rules that had logic and meaning behind them? No, of course not. Because those rules are necessary. The community could not function without them. What about the others?"

Allen said, "Lights out sucks. We all have to be in bed at 11 on weeknights. My parents stopped making me do that when I was thirteen."

"But that's about safety, too," Tamara said. "We have to be sure that everybody's in their dorm at night. And we want you to get some sleep so you'll be able to function in classes."

"Nobody does it anyway," Jen said. "Once the dorm parent isn't paying attention, people put their lights back on. As long as we're not noisy, the dorm parents never know. They don't care. They want to sleep themselves."

"Any rule that is routinely broken with no consequence is a rule that should be abolished," Sonya said. "You'll want to hold onto it for the sake of tradition, you'll want to hold onto it because it makes you feel good for some reason, but if you are truly concerned with freedom and creativity — with responsibility and, dare I say it, democracy and justice — then you won't keep a rule on the books that is unenforceable and consistently ignored."

Tamara looked like she wanted to gnaw on her arm. Jack was staring at the ceiling. Everyone else was enthralled.

Gerry, who had been silently pulling at his beard throughout the conversation, finally spoke. "What I would like to see here is more cooperation. We're all too bound by our job descriptions. The faculty only do what faculty are supposed to do, and the minute you ask them to help out with something else, they say, 'But that's not my job.' The students are the same; they expect everything handed to them. Well," he said, glancing at the students beside him, "not all of them, but I think even you guys would agree that most of the kids here just want to do their thing and not be bothered with anything that has to do with how the school functions. In general. Right?"

The students nodded.

"What I liked, Ken, about your description of the island was that it was a place where everybody knew what the basic jobs were, and they understood why they had to get done, so they all did them. They found ways to collaborate. They relied on each other. Somebody doesn't do their job, it makes life inconvenient for everyone, so nobody's going to do that. It's a kind of peer pressure. If nobody takes the trash out, the trash accumulates and starts to smell and rats come and it's a mess. So the trash gets taken out, because people don't want to live around trash. It's not a fun job, but it gets done. But I'd also bet there's not one person who's 'the trash guy' on the island. The job moves around, different people do it, it's not tied to anybody's identity. We shouldn't define each other by our work, we should define each other by who we are, and whether we're good people or not."

"I'm so glad we can all agree that being nice is a good thing," Jack said suddenly. "But you've got your heads shoved up your rear ends here. The kind of thing you're describing is one that could be taken advantage of in an instant. Anybody who felt lazy would have no reason not to be lazy. I'm as much of an anti-authoritarian as the rest of you, but this is nuts. It's masturbatory, a total waste of time." He stood up. "And now, if you'll pardon me, I have a pile of papers to read and grade."

"Why are you the only one who reads and grades them?" Sonya asked.

"What? Because I'm the teacher. It's my job. I know that's not a concept we're all happy with, but it's the truth."

"Why can't your students evaluate each other and themselves?"

"Nice in theory, rotten in practice," Jack said. "Look, I've been yacked at over the years by all the various theorists with their pedagogies of oppression and all that bullshit, I've tried all that writing process gobbledygook, and it doesn't work. Ask any alum who comes back to this school who taught them to be a better writer, and they'll say it was me. Not because I had them read their papers to each other, but because I told them when they were writing crap and I told them to stop writing crap. I got hired to be a teacher because I know something about reading and writing — maybe nothing else, but at least I know that — and so when I get up in front of a class, they know somebody with some experience and half a brain is telling it to them straight and giving them some knowledge they could use."

"Which is why," Sonya said, "you're a popular teacher. And why any student should feel privileged to have a class with you."

"Oh, so now you're trying to get on my good side?"

"Not at all. You could be a curmudgeonly old fart for all I know. I'm saying I agree with you. You've discovered a method of teaching that works for you and gets a good response from lots of students. Most teachers would be thrilled to accomplish even half of that. Any administrator who got in your way and tried to make you teach to some educational theory should be fired. You've got sound reasons for doing what you do. And I'd be surprised if students didn't feel at least a little lucky to have had you as a teacher."

Jack sat down. Grading papers could wait.

"What about a teacher who's convinced what they do is great, but in actuality it's not?" Tamara said. "What if they think hitting students is the best way to get them to behave?"

"Create the right environment and that teacher's not going to have any students for more than a day. And that's what I'm trying to get at here — it's the one real lesson I've learned from my time studying the island. Learning isn't about systems, at least not good learning, real learning. You get good learning in an environment that supports it. You get good teaching in an environment that supports it. Give up on systems; they always break down. Focus on creating the best possible environment you can, and then once you've created it, do everything you can to support it and question it to find its flaws and fix them."

"What's the difference between a system and an environment?" Sandy asked.

"That's a huge question, and I've got a plane to catch, so I'm not really going to be able to answer it for you. But I shouldn't answer it for you, even if I had the time. It's the question you should base all of your other questions on."

I thanked everyone for coming, told them we'd be meeting again, and that I hoped they would continue to think about these ideas and let me know their thoughts.

Sonya and I didn't say a word during the entire hour-long trip to the airport.

Two days later, when I tried to call her at home to let her know how positive the response to her discussion had been, she didn't answer the phone. I tried her office the next day, but the secretary of the department said Sonya hadn't come to work. I tried again a few days later. Nothing.

Mark Golden called me a week and a half after Sonya had visited the school. "You put her on the plane, right?" he asked.

"Yes."

"No-one's seen her since," he said.

CHAPTER TWELVE

From the diary of Sonya Regensberg:

Just got back from visiting Ken's school up north. Very nice place. I hadn't realized private schools came in so many shapes and colors — I guess I've still got the school from *Dead Poet's Society* stuck in my head as the prototype for them all.

It was a weird visit. Honestly, I thought I came off as a bitch. I was very cold, very composed. I was afraid of letting any cracks in my armor show, and so I pretended to be more resolved about things than I really am. I need to stop doing that. On the other hand, Ken seemed to think I was useful, and I'm glad.

He's an odd duck. Seems adrift, almost dazed, yet he's full of energy. I was probably too critical — it really does seem like a good school — but I was annoyed at how he took the island at face value, at how he seemed so entranced by the superficialities. And yet, I realize how entrancing those superficialities are. I'm still entranced a bit, myself.

Or maybe I'm too cynical for my own good. Maybe Ken's the one who's right, and I should give the superficialities a second chance. I've spent so much time in academe that I'm habitually skeptical, and yet I reread my article last night, and there's something about it, for all it doesn't say, for all it hides, that seems to get at the core of what is so magical about the island. Here's what I realized: the place is completely unpretentious.

And we don't know how to deal with unpretentious things these days. Or, at least, I don't. I spend all my time assuming anything that seems to be valuable is somehow too grand for its own good, too — oh, that word again — idealistic.

I saw a play once where one character said something like, "You may accuse me of being idealistic, but stop for a moment and realize, you're the sort of person who thinks ideals are something to be accused of."

Yes, I am that sort of person. Why?

Maybe I should go back to therapy.

No no no — follow your instincts, Sonya! I loved the island, loved the people, found the whole thing fascinating and uplifting, and yet I left full of nagging, vague doubts. I didn't want to believe in it. I couldn't believe in it.

I've been able to ennunciate some of those doubts (the limitations of environment, the difference between an educational system and a lifestyle which happens to educate, etc. etc.), but there are others that are simply *feelings*, and everybody knows I don't do well with feelings. Give me cold, hard data any day and I'm happy, but feelings — much too mushy to be useful.

Or maybe I just don't trust any of it because I'm afraid for Nick. Because I just want him to find a way to live, to find a life that provides him with both sustenance and excitement.

Do I even have that in my own life, though?

CHAPTER THIRTEEN

The next day is a blur in my mind, a storm of jumbled papers, confused phone calls, sudden conversations — doubts and worries stuffed between the rumpled clothes in a hastily-packed suitcase. What I remember most clearly are the faces of Beth and Josie as I drove out the driveway, the faces of two confused and concerned people who loved me even as I abandoned them yet again.

"I've got to do this," I said to Beth as I packed. "I'm so sorry."

She nodded, but didn't give the comforting smile I yearned for.

"How long will you be gone?" Josie asked when she saw me put on my coat.

"I don't know," I said. "It could be a couple days. It could be longer."

Tears filled her eyes and she ran to me, embracing me with all her strength. "Why can't we come, too?" she asked.

"Not this time," I said. "Maybe sometime later."

And so it was done. I was on my way to the airport to catch a late flight to North Carolina, a flight away from a thousand duties and responsibilities, the beginning of a quest for ... what? I couldn't say.

All I knew was that Sonya was missing, and for reasons I couldn't identify with any precision, I felt somehow responsible. Despite all of my responsibilities at school, despite all the time I should be spending with my family, I felt impelled to find answers to what was going on, impelled to find, if not Sonya herself, clues to where she might be — and why.

It seemed to me the only place where I might find an answer to any of my questions was the island, and so that's where I went.

***

The sea was calm as Mickey's boat ploughed through the water, scattering shards of moonlight in its wake. He barely spoke to me during the journey, and when I tried to start some small talk, he made it clear with a couple of grunts that he wasn't interested.

When we reached the island, Rob and a few others were waiting for us.

"Thanks, Mickey," Rob said, then turned to me. "Come on."

"Where are we going?" I asked.

"The Contemplation House. You need some time to think."

"Do you know what happened to Sonya Regensberg?" I asked.

"She's fine," he said.

"Where is she?"

"No more questions, Ken."

But all I had were questions, all the questions I'd brought with me, plus an endless supply of shiny new ones for every occasion.

We walked quickly along an overgrown path through the woods, avoiding the center of the island, though I could see lights shivering like infant stars beyond the trees. Twigs and leaves crackled beneath our feet, but the night was otherwise silent and still, and the loudest, most constant sound in my ears was my breathing growing heavier and heavier.

Rob opened the door of the Contemplation House for me. "Make yourself at home," he said.

"Are you locking me in again?" I asked.

"It's for your own good," he replied. "We'll see you in the morning."

I was alone. A wind picked up outside and pressed against the stone walls of the little house. The night was warm, though, and tempting as it was to light a fire in the fireplace, for I've always loved fireplaces, I had no desire to turn the house into an oven. Rob or someone had left a plate of crackers, cheese, and bananas beside a pail of fresh water, and after checking the door and all the windows to see if, by some chance, they had been left unlocked, I stopped pacing, took a few deep breaths, and sat down for a snack.

I ate some crackers and a banana, but after a couple of bites, I realized I wasn't truly hungry. I paced the room a bit, then looked at some of the books on the shelves — copies of the Bible in various translations; of Confucius; the Tao de Ching; *Zen Mind, Beginner's Mind*; *Narrow Road to the Deep North; The Gary Snyder Reader* — all predictable enough, given the apparent attempt by the islanders to create what I thought of as a kind of Zen paradise, but there were also some surprising titles: *Mein Kampf, The Prince, Das Kapital* (in three volumes! I hadn't realized it was so long, never having been much of a Marxist), various books by people whose names were unfamiliar to me, but who I learned from looking at some of the books were more or less anarchists: Michael Bakunin, Peter Kropotkin, Emma Goldman, Paul Goodman. There were numerous shelves of poetry as well, from probably hundreds of writers, some of them modern, it seemed, but many of them old and familiar names to me: Byron, Shelley,

Rimbaud, H.D., quite a few Chinese and Japanese writers, and many more.

So was this what I was supposed to contemplate? Religion, politics, and poetry?

Poetry was the only one I knew well. I'd been raised a good Protestant, gone to church and all that, but had pretty well stopped going once my life got more and more hectic, though I still held onto a concept I called "God" and kept meaning to take my family to church some Sunday. I was even less political than I was religious; though I'd always voted for a Democrat (when I remembered to vote), for the whole of my life politics had bored me, and the last thing I ever wanted to do with anyone was discuss their ideas about politicians and the political process.

Poetry, though — that's something I know well. I took a volume of Shelley down from the shelf and sat reading it for a while, until I drifted off to sleep.

When the night is left behind
In the deep east, dun and blind,
And the blue noon is over us,
And the multitudinous
Billows murmur at our feet,
Where the earth and ocean meet,
And all things seem only one
In the universal sun...

***

I woke when they opened the door, the sound of the heavy key in the iron lock piercing my sleep and erasing whatever dream had covered my mind. My back and neck ached from having slept in the chair — I hadn't woken at all during the night, or I would have dragged myself over to the cot.

Rob and a couple of other people stepped inside. In his hand Rob had a basket, and he set it on the table, opened it, and took out a plate of fruit, a bowl of some sort of cereal, and a bottle of milk. "Want some breakfast?" he asked.

"I'm starving," I said, standing up.

"Let me introduce you to some of the other Founders," Rob said. He pointed to a man with a wispy beard and a full head of unkempt red hair. "This is Will Pavan," Rob said, then pointed to a woman wearing a light brown dress that flowed around her body like a silk bandage. "And

Elise Burden." She smiled, then looked to the last person in the room, a tall, rugged man with dark skin and bat-black eyes which on anyone else might have looked menacing, but on him conveyed, at least to me, a fierce, deep intelligence. "Jack Ball," Rob said, "the wisest person on the island. He's the real founder of the place."

"How so?" I asked.

Elise said, "It was all his idea."

Jack Ball scowled slightly and said, "I once suggested it would be good to get away, and I knew a place we could get away to. That's all."

"And you told us how," Rob said, "and why."

Jack Ball sighed and took a hunk of cheese from the plate.

"Is Sonya here?" I asked, uncomfortable with the silence.

Rob put some cereal into a bowl and poured milk over it. "Want some?" he asked. I nodded and took the bowl from him.

"All of your questions, or at least the important ones, will be answered in time," Rob said. "But for now, you're just going to have to relax. We need to have a chat. A friendly chat."

The four of them gathered food and sat on the floor. I returned to the chair, but soon felt odd sitting so far above them, and I joined them on the floor.

"We're prepared," Rob said, "to offer you two choices." The other Founders nodded in agreement. "Your choices are these: We'll call Mickey and you can leave here in a couple of hours, with none of your questions answered, and having had contact with no-one else on the island. Or you can stay. But if you stay, you will need to become a regular member of the island community, not an outside observer. We don't like observers. They're useless to us."

"If I stay," I said, "then when would I be able to leave?"

"Not until we judged you to be a full citizen of the island."

"How long does that take?"

"Depends on the person," Rob said. "The shortest time I've seen it happen in was a couple of months."

"And the longest?" I asked.

Rob looked at the others. Elise said, "I think that would have to have been Adam Bellamy. About a year and a half."

"A bit more, actually," said Will.

"So you're telling me," I said, "that if I choose to stay here, I have to stay at least a couple months, maybe a whole year or even longer?"

"Yes," Rob said.

"But I have a job, a family—"

"We've given you your choices," Jack Ball said, his eyes fastening on my own.

"How much time do I have to decide?"

"Whatever amount of time you need," Elise said, though Rob's scowl made it clear he wanted me to make my decision quickly.

"Can I call my wife?"

"Yes," Rob said, "but after that, if you decide to stay, you can have no more contact with the outside until you have been judged to be a full citizen."

"So you would imprison me here. I thought you people valued freedom!"

"Our community is fragile," Jack Ball said, "and so we must protect it. We value our freedom, and because we want to see it continue we must be careful."

I stared at the floor, then raised my head, looked each of them in the eyes, and said, "Where's the phone?"

***

I can't begin to chronicle or evaluate the thoughts I had that day. With a slight change of mood, some indigestion, and a more rational frame of mind, I might not have made the choices I did. I might not have followed the Founders down the path to the village, walked behind Founder Hall, and come to the little communications shed on the north side of the island, where I called Beth and nearly ended up divorced and unemployed.

"I'm calling the cops, Ken," she said after I told her my plan. "This is insane. You've lost your mind. And I don't say that lightly."

"I have to do this," I said over and over, the only counter I had to her many logical, perfectly valid objections.

What about the kids? What about the school? What about us? Wasn't I being imprisoned, hijacked, held hostage? What did I possibly think I could accomplish?

Again and again I asked her to trust me. I asked her to talk to Helen and to Tamara and get them to cover for me, to keep the school going in my absence and to tell parents and the Board that I'd come down with a terrible illness or something, to create some excuse, to buy me some time. I needed time.

In the end, I wore her down. She had tried every argument and trick to get me to come home, but I managed to make my intentions clear, and made her think that I wasn't completely out of my head, that I was doing something important. Something worth the risk.

"Take care of yourself," she said finally, her voice a monotone, weighted down with resignation.

I turned to Rob. "I'm all yours," I said.

***

"The way the orientation works," Rob said, "is like learning a bunch of steps to a complicated dance. Each individual step has to be learned alone, just to prevent confusion, but none of the steps has much meaning without the others, so very little can be done until all the steps are put together and the dance is complete. And we even do some actual dancing together at the end of it all in celebration."

"Okay," I said. "I'm ready to learn the first step."

"You've already begun. The first step to learn is one called *time.*"

"Like the magazine?" I asked, hoping to lighten the atmosphere. Despite the fact that we were sitting on the steps outside Founder Hall on a warm, sunny day, I felt despondent, and I didn't much want to hear anything Rob had to say. I missed home, and I wondered why, only a few hours ago, I'd cut off all contact with the people I loved.

"The whole idea," Rob said, ignoring my feeble joke, "goes against everything adults have learned to value, or, at least, adults from our culture."

"What do you mean?"

"Think about your job. Time is money, right? Work faster, get more done. Be efficient. Cram more into a shorter period. Drive faster, think faster, *be* faster. Don't talk too long, don't be lazy, don't waste time. If time is a precious commodity, then wasting it is a sin, right?"

"Sure," I said.

"But what happened when you tried to just impose a bunch of ideas on your school after you returned from your first visit with us?"

"What are you talking about — did Sonya tell you about—"

"You hadn't given it enough *time*, right? You hadn't thought about what you were doing. You thought you could bring Sonya in to make things run smoothly, but she just added questions, she didn't solve anything. You were trying to impose your ideas on other people, and they weren't ready for them. They hadn't had time to adjust to a new way of thinking, and you hadn't had time to really think about what you were trying to get across."

"Okay, so I needed time. Big deal. It's hardly a brilliant insight."

"Oh, we're just beginning. Think about how you relate to the students at your school. Think about how adults in general relate to kids.

Don't you usually treat kids the way you treated the people who work at your school, imposing ideas on them, telling them you know best?"

"Sometimes adults do know best," I said.

"Of course. Plenty of times. Just as you probably had some good ideas for your school, but you couldn't put them into action because you weren't giving them enough time. It's the same with kids. Most adults try to enter into a relationship with kids by being the boss, the 'keeper of the truth'. They want to 'teach'. A perfectly good intention, but it often doesn't work out very well. Kids come from another perspective, and usually the kinds of lessons adults try to teach them end up feeling like a bombardment, like the adult is jamming ideas down their throats. So they build up resistance, the same way your school built up resistance to you as you tried to shove new ideas down their throats. The difference is, you were able to relate to your faculty and staff as professionals and adults, whereas most of the time when adults relate to kids, they try to use their advantage as adults over the kids, they try to exert power, and so they make the resistance even worse. Whereas, if the adults had given the kids more time, the lessons probably would have been learned or absorbed. But that would be a waste of time, right?"

"So if a little kid is about to run into the street and get run over, we should just tell them it's unreasonable to do that and wait for them to learn their lesson?"

Rob laughed. "Of course not. You should grab the kid and lock them inside. Kind of like we've grabbed you and locked you here for a little while."

I cocked my head, surprised by the analogy. "So where's the car that was going to run me over?"

"There were a bunch of them rushing toward you," Rob said. "You didn't see them, but I think you felt them coming, you had a certain sense of it, and that's why you came here. And why you've decided to stay."

Rob stood up. "We're going to get you into the daily routine in a few minutes, but I thought I should give some of the basic ideas to you. Most of the people who go through orientation aren't quite as intellectual as you, so we don't lay out what we're doing as clearly and transparently. But I think you'll learn more quickly if you know what we're after. At least for now."

"Right," I said quietly. "So you want me to waste some time?"

Rob smiled and said, "Only if that's what you want to do. I don't even like that phrase, myself: *wasting time*. Too many connotations of money and commodities. But look, if you want to talk about it like a manual for a corporate executive, you could say time is social capital.

Time to ask questions, to listen, to tell stories, to share the scariest thing in your life or the happiest thing. Time to experience a sunset, a sunrise, a rainfall, a perfectly clear night when all the stars can be seen. Time for experience, and time to reflect on that experience. Time alone and time together, meeting friends. Time to understand why your daughter cries herself to sleep at night."

"My—"

"And now," Rob said, "Time to learn about ordinary life here."

Rob led me across the path to one of the four buildings he called "shops", which sat beside Founder Hall. Here, he said, lots of daily work got done. "We're a model of a kind of small-time free market capitalism," he said. "We make stuff, and the stuff we don't want, we send to the mainland to have it sold."

We walked into one of the shops, which turned out to be a single room with five pottery wheels and shelves covered with pots, most of them the size of an average vase. There were bowls, cups, and plates as well, all of them the earthy pink color of clay which had been fired once and now needed to be glazed.

"Valerie's the foreman here, and she told me this morning she could use some help glazing, since some of the people who normally work here have decided to put their time this morning in the greenhouse instead."

A girl who, I thought, couldn't be more than fifteen years old came up to me and introduced herself as Valerie. "Here's your helper for the day, Val," Rob said.

"Do you know anything about glazing?" Valerie asked me.

"Nothing at all," I said.

"That's probably best."

Rob left me in her care, and soon I found myself standing in front of a table covered with buckets of glazes and rows of coffee cups waiting to be glazed.

"Play around with these for a while," Valerie said, "and then we can unload the kiln and start a new firing, and by tomorrow morning you'll get to see how they all look. Just start dipping them into the glazes. Try not to get the glazes all mixed together, but you'll definitely want to try doing layers and drippings and stuff. There's a spoon there if you need, and a couple brushes over there."

"Who made these?" I asked, gesturing to the cups.

"I made a lot of them. Various other people. A few of them will be here later, they're off doing other stuff, and we're particularly short-handed today because there's some sort of scientific study going on at the greenhouse, and a bunch of folks wanted to see it."

"It must be frustrating not to be able to depend on people," I said.

"When I need them, I tell them I need them. When I don't, I don't try to take up all their time by making them do whatever it is I'm doing. If you're working on something worthwhile, usually people will join you. If they don't, it's probably your own fault, or, as in this case, there may be something special going on."

"How old are you?" I asked.

"Fourteen. And a half."

"You seem quite mature for your age."

"Everybody here will seem mature to you," Valerie said.

"Why?"

"Because we're all responsible for our own lives. Rob always says if you took a time machine back three hundred years, back when people were being apprenticed when they were ten and became rulers of countries when they were twelve and had gotten married when they were fourteen ... well, they'd seem pretty mature. Because they couldn't afford not to be."

"Don't you think you're losing out on childhood, though?" I asked, dipping a mug into one of the buckets.

"I left my home five years ago because I was being beaten by my father, my mother was a drunk, and school was a total waste of time. If that's childhood, I don't want anything to do with it."

I set the mug on the table and dipped another one into a different bucket. Valerie sat at one of the wheels near me, slapped a hunk of clay onto it, and within a few moments a bowl had appeared beneath her fingers.

"What do you mean school was a waste of your time?" I asked.

"Learn this, learn that, do this test, do that test, blah blah blah. Even in first grade, they made sure we learned whatever they wanted us to learn every day, and they were constantly checking to see if we'd learned it the way they wanted us to, and none of it made very much sense to me, because none of it had anything to do with my life."

"But don't you think there are things you should know? I mean, shouldn't we try to create educated human beings?"

"Sure, but I just didn't want to be like every other educated human being in the class. I wanted to be whatever was most interesting for me to be."

"So now you're a potter."

"Yeah."

"Can you read?"

"Of course. I didn't learn until I was in, like, the fourth grade or something, and even then I was really bad at it, but once I got here, I *had* to read. And so I learned."

"What do you mean you had to? Do they force you to read?"

"No. I didn't pick up a book for almost six, seven months or something. I hated books. I wanted to burn them. I wouldn't go near the library. But then I wanted to know about pottery, and so I sneaked into the library when I thought nobody was looking, and I got some big books about pottery and looked at all the pictures. When the pictures weren't enough, I read the captions. When the captions weren't giving me everything I needed to know, I read the rest of the book. And then I read other books. I read a lot of Japanese poetry, too, because I had an idea to put poems into vases, kind of like the poems that are on some Japanese screens. It was interesting, and I wanted to make pots that were different from everybody else's, so I did, and when I needed to get inspiration ... well, I had plenty of places I could get it. Now I'm reading *The Tale of Genji*. Ever read it?"

"No," I said.

"It's long. It'll take me forever. But it's kind of fun. I like long books because you don't have to get to know a bunch of new characters like you do if you read lots of short books."

A fourteen-year-old reading *The Tale of Genji*. That wasn't something I'd expected to find. When I'd been teaching, it was hard enough to get kids to read modern short stories, never mind a thousand-some-odd page ancient Japanese novel. I'd also never had a fourteen-year-old make me feel under-read before. It was humiliating. And exciting.

I spent most of the morning glazing mugs and bowls, having fun dripping different glazes onto them as I got more confident (and less apprehensive about being messy). I had no idea what the bowls would look like once they were fired, and found myself surprisingly anxious to put them in the kiln.

Before we could fire the cups, though, we needed to unload what was already in the kiln, and Val and I spent a long time pulling shelves of pottery out of the huge gas-fired kiln at the back of the shop. We wrapped the pottery — mostly vases of an extraordinary variety of colors and shapes, none of them looking like the rather dull and monotonous stuff I was used to from crafts stores in shopping malls — in newspaper and tissue paper, then loaded each piece into milk crates and carried the crates to the storage barn at the other side of Founder Hall, where they would be packed and shipped to the mainland. It was good exercise, hauling crate after crate of heavy pots, and by lunchtime, I was ready not only for food, but a nap.

"I expect a bunch of people will come in the afternoon," Val said, "so you may want to find something else to do, unless you don't mind a crowd. I've sponsored a contest to see who can make the most interesting and unique teapot, and the deadline is tomorrow morning. People tend to procrastinate, but tons of people said they planned to come this afternoon to work, so..."

Val promised to fire the kiln in the afternoon, and suggested I stop by the next afternoon to see how my glazing turned out. I thanked her and headed to lunch.

I was terrified. I'd spent the morning with Val, who was wonderful, and had had a few brief encounters with other people who came in and out of the pottery studio, but I still wasn't known to most of the people on the island, and now I had to face what I assumed would be a crowd in the dining hall. Going into the dining hall at my school was one of my favorite activities, for though I tended to be so swamped with people who wanted to talk to me that I hardly got to eat anything, it was a joy to be known by everyone there, to have so many people willing to share their thoughts, ideas, experiences, and frustrations. (Though I did sometimes wish they'd be less free with sharing their frustrations, it was certainly nice to feel trusted.)

But entering a large room full of people who didn't know me was something I dreaded.

If I hadn't been so hungry, I would have skipped lunch altogether.

I was hungry, though — famished, really, my stomach churning like an old car as its engine gives out — and so I stepped into the dining hall.

It was crowded, but not as crowded as I'd expected. I got some pasta, a salad, and a sandwich, all heaped together on a plate (one of Val's, it seemed to me), and sat at a table in a corner of the room away from other people. No-one approached me, no-one stared at me, and after I'd eaten the salad and pasta, I began to feel lonely and outcast, so I took my sandwich and joined a table nearby where two young men were playing chess.

"Mind if I watch?" I asked.

"Not at all," one of the boys said. "Are you Ken?"

"Yes," I said. "You've heard about me?"

"Rob held a meeting and told the whole island about you. Jack, Elise, and Will all said they thought you were worth taking a risk with."

"Ah," I said. "I feel like a celebrity."

"You are, kind of. We don't usually let people do what you're doing. But Rob said he thinks you need us. So we voted, and a big majority said you should be allowed to be here."

"Really?"

"Yeah. We've never turned anybody away who needed us, so here you are."

I watched them play their game for a moment, then saw, across the room, leaving the dining hall, a familiar face.

It was Sonya. I was sure of it.

"Sonya!" I called, standing up, but she ignored me, and by the time I got outside, she was gone.

CHAPTER FOURTEEN

From the diary of Sonya Regensberg:

Here I am.

Nick has gone. But I'm here. Back on the island.

The doubts are all still there, but different now, even more vague. The love is still there, too, and stronger. I wanted to scream at Nick: "How can you leave this place! This is everything anybody could ever want!"

Not true at all, of course, but for some reason it's what I felt. Once I set foot on this soil again, once I saw the buildings and the beautiful lanterns, once I'd touched the plates and eaten the food again, I thought: Why would anyone leave? Why would anyone ever want more than this?

Nick didn't want to talk. "I've had it with this place," he said.

I wasn't sympathetic. I should have been. I should have talked to him more, listened to him, tried to get him to explain himself, tried to—

Instead, once again, I was selfish. Because I love it here, he has to.

No, that's not it. I was afraid for him.

This is the only place Nick has ever found stability, the only place he's ever found things to care about other than the TV or pot or trying to get laid. This is the only place where I've known Nick to be the kind of person I always thought he could be if he got beyond all the crap that held him back.

I was angry at him. I'm still angry at him. And I feel guilty for being angry at him, because I've seen all the shit he's dealt with, I've said the wrong thing more often than I've said anything right, I haven't been there for him any more than our parents, who don't even claim him as their son anymore.

I'm all he's really got in the universe, and I let him down, because I want to be here and he doesn't.

Or—

But I could go on about possibilities forever. I could live in a thousand alternate universes of possibilities, and in every one, no matter how many of the wrong words and bad moments I fixed from this world, there would still be worlds of mistakes and regrets, because nothing is perfect, and error is a human specialty.

I should get off this damned island, I should chase down my little brother, and I should help him, somehow, help him.

But I don't think I would be much of a help to him, because I don't think I ever have been. I don't think I know how.

And I don't want to leave the island.

CHAPTER FIFTEEN

I decided to spend the day observing, wandering, seeing what caught my attention. I hoped to find Sonya.

I expected Rob to intercept me at some point as I walked down the paths. I stopped at the gardens to explore the rows of tomatoes and squash, cabbage and eggplant and asparagus, beans, potatoes, rhubarb. I talked with the gardeners, who treated their work like art infused with science — the art of what to plant and why, the science of where and how. I visited the shops beside the pottery studio, shops which made jewelry and candles, a print shop which made its own paper, a woodworking studio. When I grew hungry, I went to the dining hall and made myself a sandwich. I explored the building, finding a sunny room with five people sitting at easels, painting and drawing. I discovered a small theatre where four actors practiced a scene from *The Glass Menagerie*. Outside again, in a sunny spot behind the building, a handful of people sat on the ground, talking with each other about Napoleon's decision to attack Russia, books spread open in front of them.

Later in the day, I went to see Val — went, really, to see how my glazing had turned out. She had already begun unloading the kiln by the time I arrived, and various other people filled the studio, working at the wheels, glazing bowls and cups and plates at the table, helping Val with the kiln.

She handed me a mug: dark blue, with maroon scratches like comet trails. I held the mug in the light and discovered pebbles of grey and green spackling the blue.

"Not bad for a first try," Val said.

"It's beautiful," I said. "I had no idea..."

"Keep it. As a memento."

I watched as more mugs were pulled from the kiln, mugs with more maroon or more blue, more green and grey amidst the colors, but I liked the first one the best. The beauty of a first encounter, I suppose. The beauty of surprise.

People continued to come into the studio, to crowd around each other, watching, commenting now and then. I stood beside a boy who turned a hunk of dark, heavy clay into a swirling cylinder on the wheel, then pushed the cylinder down, massaged the walls, and, finally, pulled a spout from the top edge. "I like making pitchers," he said to me. He took another piece of clay, rolled it in his hands, shaped it, and then applied it to the side of the pitcher, creating an awkward handle. His hands moved over the handle, sculpting it, until at last it seemed to have been there all along.

As the afternoon slipped into twilight, I walked out past the buildings toward fields at the edge of the island. A group of kids were playing soccer, or what seemed to be soccer, though there were no nets. I grew curious about the place of sports on the island — certainly there was plenty of space for just about any game imaginable, but how did the competitive nature of sports fit in to the determinedly cooperative spirit here?

These thoughts left me, though, when I spotted Sonya sitting beneath some trees at the edge of the field. As I approached, she noticed me, and she sat up straight, as if wanting to stand and run away, but she didn't stand and didn't run.

"Hi," I said.

She nodded.

"So this is where you've disappeared to."

"Disappeared?"

"Nobody on the mainland seems to know where you are," I said.

"Oh. Well, I told a few people. But..."

"What?" I asked. She was silent. She stared off across the field. Sunlight was drifting away, casting long shadows over the grass, washing the air with particles of grey. This was a very different Sonya than the one who had visited my school, hellbent on questioning every assumption which peeked out at her. This was, I thought, a haunted woman.

"When I got back from your school," she said, "there was a message for me from my brother, Nick. He said he was leaving the island, he was fed up, didn't want to be here anymore. He was running away. So I came here to try to stop him."

"Is he here?" I asked.

She turned away from my gaze and looked at the ground. "No," she said quietly. "They let him leave. He was here when I arrived, but they let him leave."

"And you're still here."

"Yes," she said. "I'm afraid of what I'll find when I go back to the mainland. And..." Her voice trailed off.

"What?"

"I want to know what he so hated here. It seems like paradise to me."

"Right," I said. "And who would want to escape paradise?"

We sat together on the edge of the field and watched as the day's sunlight drifted into darkness, and the clear night sky revealed the light of a thousand distant stars. It was old light, I thought, light that had traveled millions and millions of miles across a vast expanse of years, signaling the existence of stars that might now be little more than cold dust in an empty universe.

***

I didn't see Sonya again for a few days. She had a remarkable ability to disappear, though I can't say I looked for her with much effort, because Rob had an assignment for me. "I don't want you to stop doing what you're doing," he said to me at dinner. "Keep looking around, keep getting used to things here. Remember to give enough time to what you're doing for it to matter. But I want you to try something."

He paused, then took a bite of the large salad he'd made for himself.

"Well?" I said.

"I want you to try not speaking for twenty-four hours."

"Not speaking. As in, saying no words?"

"Right. Don't speak, don't talk to anybody. Don't write anything. Don't use language."

"You've got to be kidding."

Rob smiled, but he didn't laugh. "No kidding at all," he said. "Give it a try. See how long you can do it."

"Is this something other people have done?" I asked.

"Well, certain monks—"

"No, I mean here."

"What makes you think we don't have monks here? We're all monks in our own way." This time a chuckle accompanied his smile. "Just try it," he said. "Don't worry about other people."

"Okay. I'll try it. When should I start?"

"Whenever you want. Your time is yours. See what happens."

I began after dinner. I went to the room in Founders' Hall that Rob told me was to be my own — "room" is a bit too dignified of a word for what it was, "cell" is more accurate. Four walls, a window, and a bed that barely fit my body. I sat on the bed and thought about how I would pursue this task, when I would start, what I might accomplish. I knew I shouldn't try to predict the effect of being robbed of language, but I couldn't help myself. My mind raced through possibilities, and the possibility which returned to me most frequently was that I would be laughed at, scowled at, shunned. I lay down on the bed and squeezed the pillow against my ears — why, I don't know, but reason is only one element of human behavior, and seldom the most powerful.

And then I was up on my feet, ready to walk out and not speak to anyone, not write anything, not communicate. It seemed like a challenge now, maybe even an interesting one. Certainly better than lying in bed. Certainly.

***

I didn't speak or write for three days.

I listened.

It's a kind of communication, but I didn't know that before I tried.

I'd always thought of myself as a good listener. After all, didn't I have to listen to faculty and students at the school, didn't I have to listen to my wife and kids? Of course. And I did. I listened to what I thought they were telling me, and, usually, I gave them gifts of brilliant words wrapped in an aura of wisdom. I listened and responded.

Which is not the best kind of listening.

The best kind of listening, the only one that produces wonders, is *real* listening, listening without obligation, without work or preconception or self-deception. Before setting out to complete Rob's assignment, I suspect I had seldom actually listened to what people *said* — instead, I listened to what I thought they were trying to say, and, more often than not, what I wanted them to say.

Walking down the paths of the island, beginning Rob's assignment, I had no choice but to listen. My original fears were not unrealistic, and the first few people who passed me said hello, smiled, waited for my reply, and all I could do was nod and return their smile, hoping they would understand. They understood something, but I'm not sure what, because as each of them waited for some sort of spoken reply, their expressions grew more and more perplexed. One person grunted and walked on, another asked me if I was feeling well (nod, smile, thumbs up), another repeated her greeting slowly in case I was hard of hearing or new to the language.

It reminded me of a summer I'd spent in Mexico during college. I'd gone to fulfill a language course requirement (a full year of Spanish credits in eight weeks sounded like a good deal), and during the first two or three weeks, I was incapable of communicating anything except the most basic concepts: *yes, no, where is...?* The strongest memory I have of those weeks is of feeling stupid, of giving off the impression of incredible absolute idiocy, and one night at the end of the first week I lay in my bed in the little room the host family provided for me, and I cried my eyes out in frustration — *I'm a smart person with an interesting personality, and nobody knows it!* I screamed at myself. (Self-pity being one of my stronger talents.)

Now, though, I didn't feel stupid so much as alien. Of course, I'd felt alien my entire time on the island, but now I couldn't articulate my alien ideas, I couldn't smoothe the territory with explanations, I couldn't make inquiries to broaden my knowledge. All I could do was exist and observe.

During the first day of my silence, I spent most of my time in the library. I had wanted to look through the books ever since I'd first seen the building, and now seemed like an appropriate time.

People wanted to talk to me, though. I did my best not to seem rude when someone approached and asked how my visit was going, what my impressions were, what I hoped to learn. I nodded and smiled, nodded and smiled. I tried to smile less and to give subtle meanings to my nods, but the meanings were, I'm sure, so subtle that only I was aware of them.

I spent all my time in the library looking at atlases, trying to place myself in the world. The collection of atlases in the library was remarkable, including a few from the nineteenth century that made me yearn for a ship to take me to the edge of the Earth.

The building began to feel oppressive, though, its tall ceilings somehow inducing claustrophobia, the general silence burdensome when I didn't have the option of breaking it. I went outside.

The more time I spent being silent, the easier it became. People got used to me. They talked to me still, perhaps because the contortions my face made in attempts to look sympathic and interested were amusing. I *was* sympathetic and interested, even when a guy named Harry, who was making stained glass windows in one of the shops, went on for nearly an hour about the cognitive effects of light when it passed through different colors of glass.

After three days — three days of looking, of listening, of thinking; three days of hanging around in the shops and helping out a bit in the gardens and sitting in the fields — I sat down with Rob at dinner.

"Hi," I said.

"Speaking again?"

"That was the first word I've said in quite a long time."

"Good for you. How's it feel?"

"Now?" I said. "Odd. Unfamiliar. But nice."

"Wasn't so bad as you thought it would be, was it?"

"No. Pleasant, actually."

"I force myself to do it once every year or two," Rob said.

"It certainly made me realize a lot of things."

"Good. That was the point. Listening."

"Important skill."

"It's not a skill, I don't think," Rob said, "but more of a habit. One we can learn and teach, one we can lose."

"It's fascinating just to watch people."

"Did their ways of relating to you seem to change?"

"Well, I won't tell you how much gossip I've heard!"

"You were someone people trusted."

"Think they will now I'm talking again?"

"That's up to you. Listening makes you humble. Lose that humility and you lose people's trust."

"Not everybody is happy here," I said.

"I know."

"They started talking to me about it today."

"I thought they might. Eventually."

"People leave," I said. "Like Sonya's brother."

"Yes. Sometimes they come back. Sometimes not."

"There are people who don't seem to like you very much."

"I know," Rob said.

"They say you're sanctimonious, that you preach to everyone."

"Well, I probably do. Think I should do it less?"

"I don't know," I said.

I had heard the grumblings here and there, usually cast-off comments in the midst of other conversations, but two people had sought me out on that last day of my silence and talked to me about their time on the island, and their desire to leave. They seemed to think I could offer them advice, that talking to me would help them clarify their feelings. By having to express their thoughts, by creating words to fit their ideas and putting those ideas in some sort of order, they came to understand themselves better. I was just an audience, but an audience is invaluable at the right time.

The first person who talked to me was a seventeen-year-old girl named Hazel, a girl with coal-black hair that sparkled in the sun. She said she had come to the island two years ago after a fight with her parents. She'd had a friend who had come here, then left, and she didn't know where he was now, but from the stories he'd told her, she thought this would be the right place to live for a while.

"It was perfect," she said, "for a few weeks. I was dazed and happy just to be away from my parents, away from school, to have a place where

I had specific things I needed to do, and if they didn't get done, then people would be disappointed in me. Nobody'd cared enough to be disappointed in me before.

"But after a few months, I started to get kind of bored. I talked to Elise — she's always been my favorite of the founders — but she just said if I was bored it was probably my own fault, I hadn't spent enough time trying to figure myself out. I got angry with her and walked away. The more I thought about it, though, the more I thought it might be true, so I started trying to come up with interesting projects, to learn some new stuff, but there wasn't any structure to any of it, nobody seemed to care one way or another, so I just ended up bored again. I've sort of been that way ever since. It never occurred to me to leave the island until a couple weeks ago when Nick left. You know his sister, right, Sonya? Nick was totally done with this place, so he called up Mickey and got on the boat and now who knows where he is. Sonya and I talk a lot. She says the island is a finished experiment, it's got no place to go next. I don't know. All I know is, I think I'm gonna call Mickey."

Later, perhaps goaded by Hazel, a boy, Malik, found me as I was weeding one of the gardens. He started pulling up weeds, too, and after a few minutes began to speak.

"This isn't a perfect place here, you know. The founders — man, they're just nutcases. They think everything's got to be just right, we've all got to respect each other and all that. It's just crap. Do they respect each other? No way. They hardly talk to each other. Jack's getting totally fed up with it all, he's just gonna explode one day. Elise wants to be a dictator. Will hasn't got a spine, he just tells you whatever you want to hear then goes off and does the opposite of whatever it is you want him to do. And Rob. Don't even get me started. That guy thinks he's God's gift to the universe. Thinks he's got all the answers, but he's totally blind to everything that's actually going on here. So many people here, they talk some good talk, but none of them live the talk, none of them are willing to look at themselves and say, 'You know, I'm telling everybody to behave one way, and I'm not willing to do it myself.' I've had enough of it all."

I desperately wanted to ask him questions, to probe him to be more specific, to give me examples and reasons, but I feared compromising the silence, feared that the minute I spoke he would disappear.

"Every time I think I'm gonna leave, though," Malik said, "I decide it's better here than on the mainland. It's comfortable, mostly. Plenty of good people here. I guess it's just that once you think a place really has all the right stuff to be just about exactly what it should be, you have high expectations, you want it to be what your ideal image of it is. Maybe that's what I'm doing. I mean, it's not like we've got a lot to complain about, right? Little stuff seems bigger than it is. Hell, I'd miss this place. I know I would. Makes me totally frustrated half the time, though."

I didn't tell Rob the details, didn't tell him who I'd talked to, but he must have heard enough of it to know I spoke some truth.

"If people aren't happy here," Rob said, "they can leave."

"I can't," I said. "Or so you told me."

"You can leave once you've finished the orientation. You need to know what you're leaving."

I described some more of what I'd seen and heard, then said, "Every group goes through phases. You could be at the end of a phase here right now. People are getting used to things, they've lived here a while, you all know each other well — too well, probably. Maybe you need some fresh blood, some new ideas."

"We have plenty of both," Rob said. He took his dishes and cleaned them in the kitchen. I followed him, even though it was clear he didn't want me to.

"I didn't mean to offend you," I said. "I still want to learn."

Rob finished cleaning his dishes, then took mine. "You've seen a lot of the island," he said. "Now what you need to do is spend a good amount of time working in one area. Doesn't matter where. Just spend some time in one place, with just a few people. And don't forget to listen to them," he said as he walked away.

After three days of silence, the habit of listening was going to be hard to break.

***

Sonya found me later that night as I walked back to my room.

"Hazel said she talked to you," Sonya said.

"Yes."

"She's a remarkable girl."

"Seemed to be. I talked with Malik, too."

"I know him a little."

"You should chat with him. He's a fascinating kid."

"They all are," she said. "Look — I've been meaning to apologize for the other night."

"Why?"

"I was just feeling kind of depressed, sort of lost. Not very good company."

"Who requires you to be good company at every moment?"

She chuckled.

"How are you feeling now?" I asked.

"More resolved."

"About what?"

"Leaving, getting back to life. I think I'm going to write a book about this place. Rob will be furious."

"Why should he be?"

"Well, he'll *pretend* to be furious, because he likes to think of this place as a great secret. He likes it to have a mystique. But he also knows they need some publicity."

"So the island can become a tourist park?"

"That's what they've always feared would happen if too many people knew about it."

"You're right, though," I said. "If they're going to continue, they need some things to change."

"If they're going to continue, they need a lot to change."

"Such as?"

"It doesn't matter, really. Change brings new energy, new ideas. I think the foundation here, the basic stuff, is strong enough that it won't get lost. But they're just spinning their wheels right now. That's where half of the problems come from."

"And the other half?"

"Blindness and hubris," Sonya said. "They think they have the answer to how to live, but what they don't see is that everything that's successful here can only be successful here, under these particular circumstances in this particular environment."

"Why is that bad?"

"It's not bad if you recognize it. Some of them do. I shouldn't generalize so much. Maybe it's me. I mean, I keep trying to figure out what can be taken away, what are the lessons that can be learned and applied to..." She sighed. "To real life," she said.

"Spend time on things that are important and be patient. Learn to listen. Those are a couple of lessons I've started learning here. Sure, I've only learned them because the life here supports them, but I think I've learned them well enough to at least try to apply them to the outside world."

Sonya shrugged, unconvinced. "Think about your school," she said.

"I always do."

"There's not a lot you could take from here and then apply to education."

"Why not? You were the one who raised all the good questions when you came to visit. They're questions I think this place answers pretty well. Do only what is necessary, allow people the time to investigate what they want and play around and enjoy being alive."

"But if you apply all that too literally to a school, you end up losing the tension that's important to anybody learning anything."

"Why?" I asked. "If I created a school that let a kid like Val do the sorts of things she does here, how would that be doing her any sort of injustice?"

"Because Val is exactly the kind of person who has been crippled by this place. Off of the island, she'd be eaten alive. Here, she's allowed to be self-indulgent. But anybody who lives in a community larger than this can't afford to be like that. They've got to have more weapons in their arsenal."

"I don't think she's self-indulgent," I said. "I think she's motivated, she's aware of other people's needs and does her best to meet them, she—"

"You are so deluded," Sonya said. Before I could respond, she had wandered off into the darkness.

I stood outside for a while, thinking about what Sonya had said, wondering what prompted her feelings. I was tired, though, and needed sleep.

The night was quiet, but the morning was filled with chatter and shouts and the sound of people running between the buildings.

I opened the door of my room and asked a boy who ran past me what was going on.

He stopped and turned. "Mickey came. He said he found Nick on his dock." He paused, his lips trembling. "Nick shot himself."

CHAPTER SIXTEEN

From the diary of Sonya Regensberg:

I feel compelled to write, but the words shrivel at the end of the pen.

Nick.

He's alive. Yes, I can write that: Nick is alive.

I am sitting beside him in his hospital room. He is asleep. Wires and tubes run up and down his body, machines surround his bed, humming and beeping quietly. He just came out of surgery, where they removed a .22 bullet from his shoulder. They said it was small, that bullet. They said he was lucky.

If I ever questioned whether I loved him, that questioning ended the moment I got the phone call from the police.

Immediately, I thought of all the times I had criticized him, yelled at him, made him yell at me. Immediately, I regretted everything. I regret everything. I regret...

But haven't I promised myself to stop regretting? Wasn't I the one who said regret is a useless emotion, one built from what-ifs and could've-beens — yes, that's what I said, it's what I believe, and yet ... regret is what I feel.

I must move beyond regret. The present is what matters. I should have given Nick more attention in the past, but I can do nothing about the past now. I can, however, be sure to spend more time with him from now on, I can try to listen to him — to listen in a way that hears and understands.

I haven't yet been able to sleep, but I've moved in and out of clear consciousness, and in the dark half-world of exhaustion, I dreamed that Nick and I went back to the island together, that we tied up some of the loose ends and came to a point where we could rely on each other, where he could trust me as his big sister without feeling a need to push me away, and once we reached this trust we left the island together.

In truth, though, I'm not sure. I want him to wake up so we can talk, so I can find out what he's thinking. He will be filled with shame at first, shame and sadness, and I must be careful not to add to any of that. I don't blame him, really, though this surprises me. If he had died, I would probably blame him more than I do, I would be so angry at him for giving up ... but now I'm simply determined to help him, because I should have helped him before. He did this in Mickey's shop, but I know his message was for me alone.

CHAPTER SEVENTEEN

Life on the island over the next few days was both chaotic and ordinary, a surreal mix of routine tasks and extraordinary meetings, frantic encounters, and general excitement. My memory of it all is jumbled and hazy like a movie made of Monet paintings.

Nick was not dead, though that was what many of us assumed at first. He had shot himself, but had used a .22 rifle, an awkward gun to kill yourself with unless you have extremely long arms. He had tried to shoot himself in the heart by sitting on a chair, resting the stock of the rifle on the floor, putting the end of the barrel to his chest, and operating the trigger with his toe. The gun slipped and the bullet lodged in his left shoulder.

I don't know when I learned all this, and most of what I remember of that first day is running around looking for Sonya, looking for Rob, looking for anybody who could tell me exactly what was going on. Most of the other people on the island seemed to have gotten the news and were taking it in stride, glad that Nick was not critically injured but not allowing the information to draw them away from the necessary work of keeping the island functioning.

The Founders and Sonya all appeared to have vanished. I spent most of that first day asking questions of everyone I saw and getting the same answers over and over again: *Nick's fine, he's going to be okay, no I don't know where Sonya is, no I don't know where Rob is, no I haven't seen any of the Founders, no I can't really help you, sorry...*

I passed the time by helping Val at the pottery studio, lurking in the library, and weeding in the gardens. I played a couple of one-on-one basketball games at a one-hoop court beside the communications shack, demonstrating my tremendously bad shot and happily losing every game to kids who seemed, to my eyes at least, ready for the NBA.

Two days later, Rob called a meeting for the entire island. The Founders all stood at the front of the central room of Founder Hall and addressed the crowd.

"You've heard what happened to Nick," Elise said. "He shot himself, but he's going to be okay. We went out to see him, because we wanted to talk to him, to find out how he's doing, what he's thinking about, and to let him know we're not mad at him or anything. We talked a bit with Sonya, and she seems to be doing well, but we didn't get much of a chance to talk, because the police took us to the precinct station for questioning, and we've only now been allowed to leave. We hired a lawyer, because the police seemed much more interested in the island than we would like them to be. They appear to want to assign some blame for Nick's actions beyond Nick himself, and we were afraid of what they might say to family members or reporters. All Nick would say to us is that he misses life here, he doesn't feel like he matters anymore. We assured him that he is still deeply cared for and he is welcome back on the island at any time."

Somebody yelled out: "What about the police?"

"They want to visit the island," Jack said.

The room erupted. People stood, they yelled, they whispered, they screamed questions over each other. The Founders raised their arms for quiet, but it took several minutes for the noise to subside and people to return to their seats.

"We told them," Rob said, "that we have nothing to hide. We said this is a fragile community, but we welcome inquiry because we believe they will discover that in many ways we saved Nick's life before, and he will now make a full recovery because of what he learned here."

"And Sonya?" someone shouted. "What did she say?"

"She was very distraught," Will said. "I talked with her a bit, and she said she didn't know what to make of it all, but she thought she would be coming back here soon, and she might bring Nick."

I left the meeting as questions began to be repetitive and the answers were predictable. I walked slowly down the paths and found myself at the contemplation hut. It seemed like the right place to be.

Two people were in the hut when I arrived.

"I'm sorry," I said as I opened the door. "I didn't expect anybody to be here."

"Come in," said a girl I'd seen around the pottery studio. I couldn't remember her name, or the name of the girl who was with her. They were sitting in chairs, drinking tea, gazing out the window.

"I'm Ken," I said, and they introduced themselves as Cheryl and Olivia.

"Kinda crazy out there, isn't it?" Olivia said, twisting strands of long black hair around one of her fingers.

I nodded. They offered me tea and a chair.

"What do you think of it all?" I asked.

Cheryl shrugged. "We both knew Nick pretty well when he was here."

"What was he — what's he like?"

"He's nice," Cheryl said, "but he's pretty screwed up."

"Screwed up?"

"He's really angry."

"Why?"

Olivia said, "His family didn't know what to do with him, they just sort of threw him away. Sonya's been nice to him, but she hasn't been a big part of his life till recently. He just didn't know what to do with himself."

"When he was here," Cheryl said, "he struggled for a long time to trust people. He kept trying to put a wedge between himself and everybody else. He'd say stuff that was really insulting, and he'd steal things and make sure everybody knew it was him."

"Wrote swears on the walls of the library," Olivia said. "They almost kicked him out for that."

"Kicked him out?" I said.

"There's only so long you can stand a person pissing on everything you do," Cheryl said. "Excuse my language, but that's what we felt like. Like he was just pissing on us."

"What changed?"

"Rob told him he had a week to prove to us that we should let him stay here. He didn't really take it seriously before that, but then I think he got scared. I started talking with him a lot. Rob had him work in the library, and that's where I work most of the time."

"Do you think," I said, "that he was scared of being rejected again?"

"Sure," Cheryl said. "Life here can be difficult, but it's not bad. It's not as bad as what he knew. He was afraid to lose it. So once he was threatened with that, he started to try to figure out where he belonged."

"What about the lessons? The orientation?"

"Oh yeah," Olivia said, smiling. "Those." She turned to Cheryl. "Can you recite them?"

"Time, listening, sharing, experiencing, understanding, connecting, respecting. And then, depending on circumstances, leading. I've always been good at memorizing stuff."

"But does it mean anything to you?" I asked. "Why did you smile when I mentioned it?"

Olivia said, "Because it's not about what you learn or anything during orientation, it's about what you do with what you learned. I mean, okay, so Cheryl can spew off all the words. I can't. I learned them during orientation, but then I just started living the way I saw everybody else here living. It's kind of like I absorbed the words, you know? Rob's all into knowing exactly what fits what lesson and all, because he came up with it and it's important to him, but we know that being able to recite the words doesn't by itself make you a good person here, and not knowing the words doesn't make you a bad person. It's all about how you behave, really, because that's what matters. Who cares what your philosophy is, you know — what matters is how you put the philosophy into action. Beliefs are easy; actions are hard."

"She thinks the orientation is bullshit," Cheryl said.

"What about Nick?"

"He thought it was bullshit, too."

"But he did it?"

"Of course. He wanted to be here, so he jumped through the hoops and did what Rob told him to do."

"It's not that it *is* bullshit," Olivia said. "It's just that when you take a system and break it down into separate parts, it feels like it isn't relevant to anything. Then, once you've done it all, you look back and realize you're really living according to those ideas, you're holding yourself accountable to them. See, Cheryl can make fun of it all she wants, but most of what she does every day goes back to those ideas, because they're the closest things to laws that we have."

"Yeah," Cheryl said, "I wouldn't get rid of the orientation. I like it when we do the dance and stuff when somebody finishes. It's beautiful. I just ... I don't know..."

"And you think Nick needed it?" I asked.

"We all need it," Olivia said, "whether we want it or not. It isn't like the only philosophy of how to live or anything, but if you keep reminding yourself of those lessons, you'll be a better person than you would be otherwise. It's just that nobody really wants to try to be a better person all the time. We'd rather just live."

"Exactly," Cheryl said. "The island lets us do that because we all have the same basic ideas about what respect is and how we should treat each other."

"Then what happened to Nick?" I asked.

They were silent for a moment, until Olivia said, "He forgot the rest of the world hasn't been through the orientation."

***

The next morning, I found Rob and said, "I'm ready for the next step. Which one is it?"

Rob was talking with Elise and Jack outside Founder Hall. He laughed at me. "It's not like learning algebra."

"What do you mean?"

"Why don't you spend some time with Jack and get him to tell you about what he thinks of the lessons. We've got work to do."

Rob and Elise quickly disappeared down one of the paths and I was left standing with Jack, his face placid and his eyes focused intently on me. I was sure he thought I was the most ridiculous person he had ever seen.

"Well," I said, hoping to break the awkward silence. But I couldn't think of anything else to say.

"Rob is angry," Jack said. "He's scared."

"What's he scared of?"

"Change."

"Oh," I said. Jack began to walk away from the building and toward the fields. I followed, though I didn't think he wanted me to.

As we came close to the field, Jack spoke again. "I told him I thought we had accomplished everything we set out to accomplish, and that it is time for us to leave the island. Leave it to the people who are here, let them make of it what they will. We are no longer needed, if we ever were."

He walked into the field and gestured for me to follow.

"I told him what happened with Nick was a wake-up call to us. We need to go out into the world, we need to figure out ways to bring the island to the mainland and the mainland to the island. If we don't, then all we have created is a prison, and all we are doing is helping people into helplessness."

"Do you think the lessons do that?" I asked.

"No. We created them over time, over many long conversations, and they were helpful to us when we continued to talk about them. When we stopped the conversation and wrote the words in stone, then we lost the most important part of what we had learned."

He held his arms open to the soft breeze. "Look at this field!" he said. "So many possibilities! So much you could do in this space! Bring me a baseball and we'll play a game, bring me a costume and I'll make a play, bring me a hammer and I'll build a house — this is what life should be — an open field!"

He sat down and rested his head in his hands. "I'm going to have to leave soon," he said. "I don't know anything except the island."

"Why isn't that enough?" I asked.

"It was for a long time. But it's not enough for a life." He smiled at me. "Which lesson are you on, do you think?"

"Well, I've done time and listening, so..."

"Experience. A good one. Take time to listen and eventually you'll begin to experience things, things you wouldn't have experienced otherwise. Observation becomes action. 'Be in the moment,' isn't that what people say? *Carpe diem.* Experience. Sometimes I think it should be last, because it's the most difficult lesson, the most abstract and fragile. It never ends. But none of them do. That's what makes it all so hard." He flung his arms out and flopped down on the grass. "Sometimes you just want to lie in a field and watch the clouds move over you and not think about life or philosophy or other people. Don't you?"

"A lot," I said.

"Then lie down. Lie down!"

I lay near Jack in the grass and squinted as the sun moved out from behind a cloud.

"Twenty years from now," Jack said, "how will you remember this moment?"

"I—"

"Not in words. Don't give me words. Just think about it."

And so I began to think: What was I feeling now, how did my body touch the ground, how did my eyes notice the light, what did my nose discover in the air, what sounds (birds, distant voices) took my attention from my thoughts...

"Experience," Jack said. "It starts with yourself, and eventually, after a lot of practice, you begin to be able to understand other people's experiences, too. At least, I hope so."

My stomach churned and I realized I hadn't eaten breakfast. The grass beneath me was damp. Sunlight washed across the sky and I squinted, focusing on the blue behind the blinding light. The air hung thick with the smell of the sea, and a bird whose cry I couldn't identify called *whick whick whick* in the distance.

***

I found Rob when I went to the dining hall to make something for breakfast. He sat alone at a table toward the back of the room, and I brought my bowl of granola and milk over and asked if he would mind me joining him.

"Have a seat," he said. "I've got a new assignment for you."

"I feel like James Bond," I said.

"Not quite so much fun, unfortunately. How'd it go with Jack?"

"Fine," I said. "He's an interesting guy."

"Yes."

"We talked about change. He seems to think this place needs some shaking up."

"That's what he keeps saying. We need to be dynamic, not static. That's what he thinks. Do you agree?"

"To some extent," I said. "People don't learn much in a static environment."

"True. It's a new problem, because until now everything has just been so fragile that any change was a threat. We never had one day where we could say we were really doing everything we wanted to do."

"And now?"

"Now," he said, "we've gotten good at doing all the basic things, and we don't know where to go from here. We've got so much potential, but we're so afraid of losing it that instead of making any sort of choice of where to go, we keep doing what we've always done and hoping the future will work itself out. Maybe it will."

"Maybe," I said. "Can you afford to bank on maybe?"

"I don't know." Rob sighed, then said, "But we should talk about what's up next for you. Here's what I want you to do: Go meet someone you haven't met yet, and walk down to the beach with them. Come back and shoot some hoops or something. Then come see me again."

"That's it?"

"That's plenty," Rob said.

***

I used to be shy, but I've had to get over it. As a child, I hated meeting new kids, because I was always afraid they would think I was strange or annoying. It was easier just to hang around with people I already knew, or to avoid people completely and hide behind a book. Books were my escape and refuge, and they often still are — nothing relieves stress for me more than an hour or two with a book by a favorite author.

Of course, becoming a teacher forced me to interact with many people I didn't know. Every year a new crop of students, and even at a small school there are always kids you haven't encountered before. I didn't mind the students so much as I did their parents: I procrastinated on phone calls to parents about their children, I hated Parents' Weekend more than any other time of the year, and after hours and hours of parent-teacher conferences I went home as soon as possible, unplugged the phone, turned off all the lights, and hid. I tried my best to communicate with parents, but always felt intimidated, afraid they would accuse me of harming their child, afraid they would question my reasons for teaching, afraid they would tell me I didn't know anything I was talking about.

Then I became a headmaster and it got worse. I simply had no option to be shy; students, parents, alumni, and hundreds of strangers pressed their way into my life, and, slowly, I learned to enjoy them. I traveled constantly trying to fundraise, and if there's anything a shy person really hates, it's asking people for money. But I believed in what I was doing, and I felt that what I was doing would help people, so I got through the first few awkward fundraising events and discovered myself excited to go on the next trip, to challenge myself to be honest and eloquent enough to get a big gift from a major donor. I enjoyed learning to be comfortable when surrounded by people at parties, I enjoyed meeting parents and talking to them about their child's experience. I enjoyed meeting students most of all, even the ones I had to meet with to tell them they would not be welcome at our school anymore. I set myself the goal of making every expulsion an opportunity for both of us to learn something, and though I certainly haven't always accomplished that goal, aiming for it has kept me both honest and passionate.

So now when I was faced with finding someone I didn't know and convincing them to spend some time with me, I shouldn't have been as scared as I was. I had accomplished far more difficult tasks in my life, and yet now I was terrified — how could I possibly go up to someone and ask them if they wanted to walk down to the beach and then play some basketball? They would think I had escaped from the state prison.

I needed to come up with a goal, a reason to spend time with someone. As I began trying to think of a reason, it occurred to me that my thinking was absurd. Why was I afraid simply to spend time with someone I didn't know? Not because I didn't have a goal, but because I didn't know how they would react to me. That was what mattered most in my mind: my effect on someone else.

When I realized this, I was appalled. Shouldn't I be able to live without always dwelling on what other people think of me? Surely a man as educated as I am, as experienced in the world, as accomplished and successful — surely such a person should not have to worry about what other people think!

And yet I did. I was still the little kid afraid other people would think him weird or annoying.

Now I was angry. I had thought I was better than I was, thought I had outgrown the self I so disliked, the self that held me back and kept me cowering, hiding from the world.

I marched to the gardens, saw a boy I hadn't noticed before, and said, so quickly I wasn't sure my words sounded like English, "I haven't had a chance to see the beach here yet. Would you mind showing it to me? We could shoot some hoops on the way back."

The boy looked me over, cocked his head, smiled, and said, "Yeah, just let me finish planting this."

***

We walked on the path between the upper and lower fields and past a pond I'd never paid any attention to. A couple of ducks floated on the pond, trailing tiny waves behind them. Past the pond was another field, beyond which a hill rose.

"I'm Ken," I said to the boy as we walked along. "What's your name?"

"Arturo," the boy said. "People just call me Art, though. I'm gonna change my name someday, but I haven't decided what I want to change it to."

"Why are you going to change your name?"

"It just doesn't sound right. Besides, it was my dad's name, and I don't get along real good with him. So I'm gonna change my name.

As we stood beside the pond, Arturo said, "Have you seen the sculpture garden?"

"No," I said. "Where is it?"

"On Lighthouse Hill. Come on." He sprinted across the field and up the hill.

The top of the hill gave a clear view not only of the island, but of the ocean beyond. I could see why the beach on this side was named Long Beach: it began near the pond and stretched past the field and the hill, ending in craggy cliffs at the western tip of the island.

Lighthouse Hill got its own name from a boulder into which rough steps had been carved and a lantern planted. Every night, Arturo said, someone came and lit the lantern, and every hour someone else checked to make sure it was still burning.

"Can boats really see it?" I asked.

"Probably not," Arturo said, "but people think it's a good thing to do anyway. We talk about it at meetings a lot. It feels like an honor to light the lantern and check on it, so nobody really wants to stop."

He led me past the boulder to a flat area exploding with flowers. A young man and woman sat on iron benches in the garden, talking. Sculptures of stone and metal lurked between the flowers like gnomes.

"Who makes the sculptures?" I asked.

"Anybody who wants to," Arturo said.

I said hello to the two people on the bench, and they smiled at me. Clearly, Arturo and I had stumbled on a romantic get-away, but the couple didn't seem unhappy that we had found them.

The flowers stunned me with their color, but I was most interested in the sculptures, which didn't seem to follow any particular style or form other than what the artist felt like creating at the moment they had created it. And yet each sculpture demonstrated great skill: an egg-shaped stone balanced between two metal hands, a pyramid of thin wires which swirled into the shape of a woman in the center, a sharp-edged stone nearly as tall as me that zigged and zagged at every inch so much it seemed out of focus.

I could have stayed in the garden for hours, but I already felt guilty for taking so much of Arturo's time. Surely he had better things to do than wander aimlessly with me.

We walked down the hill and to the beach. The sand was hot.

"Want to go swimming?" Arturo asked me.

"I'm not wearing a bathing suit," I said.

"Just wear your shorts. They'll dry quickly enough."

I chuckled, took off my shirt and shoes, and raced Arturo into the water. We rode the waves like befuddled jellyfish and threw water and mud at each other. Finally, exhausted, we climbed out of the water and settled in some grass just beyond the beach.

"That was fun," Arturo said. "Thanks for bringing me."

"I should be thanking you. Why did you say yes when I asked you to come down here?"

"Because I hadn't been here for a while, and I was getting bored at the garden."

"Do you get bored here a lot?" I asked.

"Not really. There's plenty to do, plenty of stuff that needs to get done. I just haven't found anything that really excites me yet."

"How long have you been on the island?"

"A few months, I guess. I don't know. Eight months. Yeah. Maybe nine."

"Don't pay a lot of attention to time?"

"Most of the days are similar around here. We do the dance every month or so, and that's a nice change, and sometimes people go back to the mainland to do some sales or something, but I haven't had a chance to do that yet."

"But you like it here?"

"Sure. It's better than anywhere else I've been."

"Where have you been?" I asked.

"I was born in Brooklyn, and I lived there for a while, then my mom got a job teaching at the university down here, so we moved, and my mother thought it was just better for me to be on the island."

"Did your mother decide that?"

"No, but she was okay with it. She always wants what's best for me. She's really smart and everybody respects her, so she got me to go here."

"When did you last talk to her?"

"I call her once a week just to let her know I'm okay. She cries and says she loves me. She loves me a lot."

"Does she want you to come home?"

"No," Arturo said. "She says I should come home in a couple months and we can see how things go. She loves me, though."

"She doesn't mind that you're not in school?"

"She thinks it's weird, but I got in trouble at school a lot, and here I don't, so she doesn't mind. She told the school I'm living with my dad now, back in Brooklyn."

"When did you last see your father?"

"I don't remember," Arturo said.

We sat together on the edge of the beach for a while, until I said, "You up for a game of basketball?"

"Sure," Arturo said, and we ran together back to the basketball court, where a variety of balls — soccer balls, red playground balls, baseballs, beachballs, and even a couple of basketballs — sat in a large plastic box for anybody to use. Arturo and I played against each other for a while, with Arturo easily beating me by nearly ten points, until a few other people arrived and we created teams. This time, Arturo and I were on the same team, and I did my best to stay out of his way, though many of the other players were better than he was. Basketball has never been my sport.

***

I found Rob at dinner, sitting with Elise and Will.

"It was a good day," I said. "A good experience. And since, presumably, that's the lesson I'm on, it's been effective."

The Founders smiled. "You've cracked our code," Elise said.

"Ran into a couple of girls who told me about it. Time, listening, experience ... actually, I don't really remember the rest."

"Don't worry about it," Rob said. "Call it anything you want — the labels don't matter. The ideas and behaviors are important, though."

"I spent most of the day with Arturo," I said. "I'm completely exhausted."

Elise said, "Nothing wrong with that."

"Arturo's a great kid," Will said. "Horrible situation."

"Yes," I said, "he told me a little bit about it."

"Mother's a heroin addict, father's in prison for murder. They were living on the street just before he came here."

"What?" I said. "He told me his mother worked at the university."

Will frowned. "He tells people something different about her every day. Last time I talked to him, his mother was going to Washington, D.C. to work for the president."

"He kept saying his mother loves him."

"Yes," Elise said, "because he has to keep reminding himself. She never tells him."

I stared at the immense salad on my plate, but didn't feel much like eating it.

"Don't get too depressed," Rob said. "You and Arturo had a good day. At some point, you'll probably be able to talk to him about what's really happened in his life. But neither of you are ready for that. You need to have some more experiences, you need to spend some time experiencing the world through his eyes, and he needs to see a bit through yours. If you two put in the time, you'll get to a point where you've had enough experiences together to be able to trust each other. Trust isn't something you can force, it's not something that just suddenly appears. We all lie to each other to a certain extent, just like Arturo lied to you. His lie seems awful because of the reality we know is beneath it, but I'd rather have Arturo's lies, lies which he needs for protection, than all the silly lies we throw at each other each day without even noticing."

I nodded, trying to agree. I still felt wretched, as if I should have known there was more to Arturo than I had noticed. What good is spending most of your life around kids if you don't see beneath their words? Had I been this blind with students at my school? Had I never truly known the worlds they walked through?

THE LAST CHAPTER

I had worried that waiting two years to return to the island was too long. I had also worried that it was not long enough.

My life had changed significantly after I returned — I left the school, unable to feel comfortable within the confines of a traditional boarding school life, unable to match my vision to the structures around me. I separated from Beth, saying goodbye to decades of memories. For weeks and months afterward, I tried to figure out how to live on my own without the job I was used to have to fill in every moment of my day, without the person I had spent so many of those, and other, moments with. So much of my life seemed to have disappeared from me, to be the life of someone I read about or saw on TV, not a life I had lived. I couldn't have been that person, could I? But who was I?

Ruth and Josie saved me. Good friends saved me. I had spent years talking about developing honest and valuable relations with adolescents and children, I had learned all the lessons of the island, the lessons of listening and unconditional love, but talk is one thing and life is another. Few of us ever live up to our talk all the time, and I certainly didn't. I stopped even listening to myself, never mind listening to other people. But as I sat with Ruth and Josie in a house we were renting, a house with barely any furniture and a lot of boxes full of hastily-packed who-knows-what, we shared fun memories, memories of building sand castles on a beach in Maine one spring when the ocean was far too cold for swimming but the sand was perfect for making castles; memories of baseball games played and watched; memories of birthday cakes and Halloween costumes and playing hookey from school to go fly fishing; memories of telling jokes and ghost stories and fairy tales. We used these memories to reconstruct the stories of who we were, and who we wanted to remember to be.

I had friends who should have been angry at me, and I'm sure they were. I was a wreck, and I wanted company in my wreckage. I no longer knew why I was running a school, why I was a husband and a father, why I was trying to do or be anything. Who was I? Nothing added up, and I couldn't reconcile the world in my head with the world around me. My best friends realized this. They couldn't solve anything, but they could offer their presence. A hug, a slap on the back. A late-night phone call just to say hi. An invitation to dinner or a movie or a ballgame. Stories of their own lives to distract me from mine, to offer sympathy and commiseration. A willingness to listen to all my blather, even when it didn't make much sense, even when all I was trying to do was keep talking so that I'd know I still existed.

And I made it through. *This, too, shall pass*, I kept reminding myself. It may be a cliché, but we need clichés at our worst times, because their familiar wisdom is more comforting than the strangeness of originality. Josie insisted that I learn how to cook, because she said just because she was the only woman still living with me full-time didn't mean she was going to do all the cooking and cleaning. (I told her she still had to clean her room. She said she would if I'd clean mine. It was a fair deal.) Friends got me some consulting jobs so there was at least a bit of an income, and I got to travel, which pulled me out of myself and helped me remember how large and varied the world is. I don't know if I offered anyone any useful advice, but I got the chance to think more about my ideas, to process what I had learned on the island, and to think about what was important.

And eventually I got another job, this time one that seemed perfect: to start a school from scratch. To figure out how to make the lessons of the island practical, real, something we could put into everyday practice in the real world. We're just beginning. I'm a little scared, certainly, but also excited, refreshed, rejuvenated. Alive.

After I got the offer of the new job, I decided to visit the island again before accepting. All of the kids were gone, dispersed through the world, the island empty and abandoned, a dream or an experiment or a memory that had done what it needed to do and had drifted away afterward. I asked Sonya and Nick to meet me there, and invited Ruth and Josie to come along as well.

We met at Mickey's. He wasn't there, but he'd left us a boat. The water was remarkably still as we moved across it, and twilight turned the world around us into a pencil drawing.

We talked to each other in the boat — I told Sonya and Nick all that had happened to me, Ruth told them she had graduated from college and had found a job working at an advocacy group for homeless people in Boston, Josie said she had decided that she had probably been onto something when in the first grade she'd told her teacher she wanted to be an astronaut. Sonya was still teaching, and Nick was working as the manager of a record shop in Florida and thinking about going to community college or maybe Africa, because he'd gotten interested in African drumming.

But when we arrived at the island, our words and stories stopped. We walked up the path from the dock without speaking at all.

We turned the corner and walked toward the village, but something was wrong. It took a moment for me to notice.

"Oh my god," Sonya said.

"It's gone," Nick said.

I couldn't speak. All of the buildings had disappeared. The path ended. The gardens, the lanterns — everything was gone. Only grass and trees remained. As if the island had never been built on. It had been less than two years since everyone had left, but now it looked as if no-one had ever been here at all. Surely it couldn't all have been taken away in such a short time? I could barely breathe.

We kept walking. No library, no Founders' Hall. Nothing. Trees and grass.

In the darkness, we separated from each other. We wandered as if entranced, in a daze. I knelt down in the field and ran my hands through the grass and dirt searching for something, anything, some relic or sign.

A breeze blew. From a distance came the sound of drumming, soft at first, then louder, carried by the wind. I stood up. A light flickered somewhere ahead of me, indistinct and mysterious, like a campfire in a fog. I walked toward it, and the light became clearer. It was, in fact, a fire, but a big one, a bonfire.

As I approached, the scene grew familiar. I remembered it. Or I remembered dreaming it. The drumming was louder now. Other instruments joined in, guitars and trumpets. It sounded like some sort of reggae music, something with a deliberate beat, something people could dance to.

And they were dancing. The islanders — everyone I had met. They wore clothes they had made themselves, clothes painted and dyed with swaths and splashes of color that rippled in the fire's light. The music swung against their bodies like a current of water, like drifting smoke.

Faces appeared and disappeared in the shifting light. I recognized them and they recognized me, but names abandoned me — we were not names, we were something else, something beyond whatever had been ascribed to us by words. I remembered where I had known these faces before, the various moments of my life that had been watched by these eyes, moments when I was young and moments later, moments when I had been at my best and moments of my worst. Moments of experience.

The music continued to press against us, and I discovered I was moving with everyone else, my body suddenly light, my steps assured.

Dancing, not galumphing. Swirling. Were my feet still on the ground? Had I transformed into air?

It occurred to me that I could be dead and this was Heaven. "Good job, God," I said. "This is just the Heaven I wanted. More than I deserve, really." But somehow I knew this wasn't Heaven, that it was both more and less real than that.

Hands met, arms entwined. We circled around and through each other, the music propelling us. We danced together and apart, every person moving forward and back to everyone else, a kaleidoscope of faces and dreams. Some people smiled, others did not, but I knew there was an energy here that came from how much we cared for each other, how much we needed each other to keep ourselves from stumbling, from falling, from losing the rhythm. A kind of love, and unconditional, necessary, the basic element of survival.

I understood these people, but I could not explain what I understood — it was too big, too amorphous. I felt the understanding was returned, and it wove us together just as the music did.

We listened not only to the music, but to the rhythms we each danced to, the individual steps adding up to a unique whole. I realized, then, that we were each leading the dance, that it had no one leader, but yet it was led because all of us were listening to each other, feeling our way across the landscape and through the shadows, listening carefully and honestly, understanding. Time slipped away, because we had all that we needed, an entire eternity to share and experience.

"Ken?"

I turned and saw Sonya's face in the moonlight, felt her hand on my shoulder.

"We should probably head back," she said.

Silence surrounded us. The fire had disappeared, the dancers had dispersed. Had they been there at all? Had they ever been there?

"Did you ... see anybody here?" I said, my words whispers.

"No," Sonya said. "It's abandoned."

"You didn't hear anything?"

"What do you mean?" she said.

"Music ... or something?"

"No. The quiet's kind of eerie."

Indeed, it was eerie. Absolute silence, no sound at all. And then, suddenly, the sound of trees touching each other in the wind, the sound of waves washing against the island's shores.

"Where are the kids?" I said.

"Nick's telling them stories. They're entranced."

"I meant the islanders."

"They're gone, Ken. They went back to where they came from, or to places they'd never been before. New lives and old lives. Remember?"

"I remember ... something," I said.

"Come on. We should get some rest."

"Wait," I said.

"What?"

I looked into her eyes, and they seemed new to me then, as if I'd never seen them before, so blue and sharp and bright. "I wanted to ask you — I mean, I've been meaning to ask you — earlier, I was going to ask—"

"Yes?"

"I'll need some help with this new school. And, I thought, maybe, well. You're the best person I could have to help me with it. You'll keep me honest. So if you want. If you need some work. If you were interested in doing something new. I thought. Maybe..."

Sonya laughed. "It's about damn time you asked! I thought you thought I must be some nutcase or something!"

"And I thought you'd think I was the same, so I've been terrified to—"

But before I could finish saying anything, she grabbed me in a hug and kissed me. She took my hand. "Come on," she said. "The kids are waiting. We've got a lot of work ahead of us."

I smiled and felt tears grow in my eyes. We found Ruth and Josie and Nick sitting at the dock, dangling their feet in the water while Nick told them all about the island and his time there. We climbed into the boat.

As we sailed away from the island, I didn't let myself look back. I knew the island would be disappearing in the darkness, and I was afraid that if I looked back I might imagine I saw a light there. But as Sonya took my hand and I listened to Nick continue telling Josie and Ruth about how people should trust and challenge each other, should care more deeply for each other, should care about the lives they led, I imagined all the lanterns from the island spread out across the world, casting moments of light and calling us all to remember how well we might dance together.

DANCING LESSONS

Dance steps

Unconditional love

Time
Listening
Experience
Understanding
Mutual Understanding
Lead

We all want to be understood and feel connected to others. In our relationships we can have a powerful effect on each other, especially during critical periods such as adolescence. We are all unique and want others to understand who we are as individuals. This process of seeking uniqueness, being understood and being connected occurs throughout life but has a particular significance during the second decade. As children enter the second decade of their lives, they develop a desire to discover their uniqueness at a time when the significant adults in their lives -- parents, teachers, family, coaches play important roles in shaping adolescents into productive and contributing adults in the larger society.

Traditionally the adult-adolescent relationship is viewed as a struggle of power with the adult owning the power. This view has some legitimacy -- however, if it is the only way of relating, it is limited and ultimately undermines the long-term health of the relationship.

The Dance

An interesting way to view this relationship is through the metaphor of a dance, with each partner possessing a unique and mutual role in the experience. As in a dance, power can be viewed less from a controlling standpoint and more from a wisdom standpoint.

Wisdom-as-power provides the leader with the ability to know what is needed at any given moment. Viewed from this perspective, the powerful dancing partner understands when to lead, when to follow and when to enjoy the mutual flow. When power is viewed as possessing more wisdom, more understanding, a deeper ability to listen, then the leader is in a more powerful position to shape and direct the outcome. This is not an abdication of control or power -- actually quite the opposite. This way of relating definitely takes more time, is more frustrating and at times messy, but the long-term results are deeper and more satisfying.

Obviously, this view of human development does not mean that an adult should ever let a child endanger themselves or others. But again, this is where wisdom and experience would overrule. And if the relationship is built on mutual trust and understanding, the adolescent will ultimately be more motivated to listen to reason. More important, authoritarian power relies heavily on guilt and authoritarian presence.

Ultimately what we are trying to cultivate is intrinsic motivation -- the desire to do the right thing even in the absence of an authoritarian figure. Like a dance, however, both partners possess the wisdom at different times. If the adult has built a relationship founded on time, listening, understanding and trust the adolescent will be intrinsically more willing to align herself with the right course. The beauty of a mutual dance is that it is each partner's responsibility to guide the relationship.

Partners in Life

The basic idea of a mutual dance is that each partner enters the relationships on equal footing. They both share the same music. This is where many adults have a difficult time. The most common response is "why should we enter on equal footing? We are not equal -- the adult is the one who has the power and responsibility."

In one sense this is true. Ultimately it is the adults' responsibility to raise, teach and coach the adolescent. The amount of experience alone would suggest that the adult is the keeper of the power.

However, it is the way in which we relate to our younger partners that makes the subtle difference. If we enter the relationship simply by stating we are the boss with all the power, then the relationships is built on that power structure.

If, on the other hand, the relationship is built on mutual trust, commitment and responsibility the adult is in a position to teach from the right platform -- wisdom and experience. Equally important, the adolescents know this, respect this, and will ultimately "buy in" to our important lessons.

A Matter of Respect

There are many unnecessary ways adults show their children, students and players that they are not equal.

Most adults do not talk to or treat the teenagers the same way they do their friends and colleagues. I can tell, for example, when an adult answers the phone precisely who they are talking to -- their children or a mutual friend. The tone of respect is different. Is this necessary? Does it matter? Ask your adolescent. Adolescents pick up on the difference. In this sense, the adult has established an unnecessary relationship of power through a seemingly unnoticeable venue.

Another way adults create an unnecessary we/they relationship is when they talk publicly about their children and students in the third person. I have sat in thousands of teacher-faculty-student meetings where I can tell immediately which parents and teachers have the healthier relationships. Instead of providing the adolescent the opportunity to represent their own feelings and thoughts, many well-meaning adults provide a synopsis of the adolescent's views. This has a powerfully negative impact on the relationship. All one has to do is glance over at the adolescent while the adult is "giving an overview of them" to see the disappointment and disgust.

The Power of Relationships

The power that the adult has resides in their wisdom, maturity, experience, and ability to understand their role in the relationship.

First, adults need to understand their adolescent partners as legitimate philosophers. This does mean the adolescent is right; it simply means they have a legitimate point of view that deserves understanding and respect. This does not mean that adults need have to comply or agree. But they do need to convince the adolescent that they have listened and they understand and respect their point of view. The power that adult possesses is the power to give adolescents the safety and freedom to empty their emotional well. The reward can be enormous.

The adult's role is to create a safe environment void of criticism and guilt where adolescents can share their true feelings. Sometimes that means that adult simply needs to listen and understand—truly understand. Once the adolescent is fully understood than the mutual dance of learning begins. The adult now possesses the authentic power to lead.

As adolescent experiment they begin to learn for themselves and they can come to the adult and share their feeling. If the adult is simply the authoritarian who owns all the power, the adolescent will be less likely to share their feelings. They may comply out of fear. The better motivation for taking the right road is that they do not want hurt the relationship.

The concept of "Dancing with the Natives" is founded on the power of relationships and the belief that people are innately good and want to do good. The adult's power is located in the ability to spend time, to listen, and to display an authentic desire to understand. In turn, we develop a new power that allows us access to the adolescent world and the keys to shape their lives in a powerful and enduring way.

As the famous song goes, we teach our children and our children teach us -- that is the dance. *Dancing with the Natives* is about the beauty and struggle of adults' relationships with their younger adolescent partners. As Ray Charles told Jamie Fox in preparation for playing him in the film Ray, "the notes are right below your fingers all you have to do is play the right ones." So it is with our relationships.

How adolescents think, feel and live their lives; how their rituals, music, and peer relations create a sort of sui-generis world -- a culture of their own deserves respect. A culture that completely confuses most adults. When given unconditional love, a little time, understanding and the freedom to express themselves, adolescents' inner beauty will flourish.

Too often children entering the second decade of their life are viewed as aimless and unable to make healthy decisions. When shown unconditional love and the genuine opportunity to govern their environment they are very respectful and responsible—for the most part. This is not to say they are always right or that adults should abandon their love, views and interest in helping but it does mean that when given unconditional love in time adolescents develop a sense of trust and ultimately want to do good.

To dance is to relate. To relate, to truly relate, requires time to learn the lessons the adolescents have to offer.

The Dance Steps

When we think of dancing, at least metaphorically, we think of rhythm, flow and a mutual connection to shared music. The same is true with the "Dancing with the Natives" analogy. A dance requires trust, time and practice. So do relationships. When we first learn a new dance we need to begin with the essential steps that provide the foundation for the more complex moves that will follow. And so it is true with our relationships with adolescents. Although all the steps are essential there is a sequence to the steps. The learning of one step leads to the next and with time the dance evolves into a more complex and meaningful dance.

The biggest mistakes adults make is to negate the values and importance of the early steps. Many adults say to themselves, "I know what is right, I have been there, I am older and wiser and I know what you need to do."

Some of that may actually may be true. But the reality is that that forcefulness will at best create compliance, but it may also silence the beauty of the deeper dance of life.

Naturally, all of the steps are engaged in simultaneously and continuously, but the sequence builds and deepens the relationship in a natural way. The important point is to try and suspend the tendency to tell, direct, control and lead until a solid relational foundation built on unconditional love, time, experience, listening, understanding have been solidly formed.

The first step to *Dancing with the Natives* is **unconditional love**. Without unconditional love there is no foundation. Without unconditional love the whole dance falls apart. Unconditional love means that we accept and love our partner the way they are and that we in fact love them for who they are and we do not want to change them.

Time follows unconditional love and provides the venue for solidifying the relationship, particularly in the early stages of the relationship. Time provides the opportunity to develop a shared history. Time allows each person to get to know one another, to share experiences, tell stories, understand each other. Beginning with unconditional love and sharing time one can begin to listen, truly listen.

Authentic listening allows the adolescent to feel comfortable enough to empty their emotional well and share their inner self. Authentic listening is difficult for adults who have an agenda and are waiting to dispense their self-proclaimed important life lesson. Adolescents know immediately if the adult is an authentic listener.

Experience is next. Experience means sharing experiences together. Listening to music, going on road trips, meeting each other's friends, walking in the field, sitting by the fire, attending a concert together, spelling the flowers and skiing. Experience creates a whole new category of shared feelings, sights, memories, sounds and smells that connect to the mind, body and soul and serves to represent the relationship. Experience extends and deepens both the relational memory and shared history.

Understanding naturally flows out of listening and experience and provides both the adolescent and adult with a natural opportunity for connecting. Understanding is not judging. Understanding is allowing the adolescent to be their own philosopher. Understanding leads to mutual understanding. This is when the adult has spent precious time learning the foundation steps and now shares with the adolescent their feelings, views and thoughts. The adult begins to develop a mutual relationship, sharing with their partner how they see the world. The adolescent is now emotionally prepared to spend time in the mind and heart of the adult. Although this will happen throughout the dance, the basic theme of *Dancing with the Natives* is to build this sense of trust so they are ready to receive the leadership and direction and wisdom the adult has to offer.

Like the remote islanders, adolescents need time to trust the outsiders and the outsiders need time to understand the feelings, philosophy and rituals of the native culture. It is now time to **lead** and the real beauty and magic of the process is moving beyond compliance to intrinsic motivation on our partner's part and to accept (and dance with) the adults' wisdom, guidance and direction.

To dance, truly dance with another person is a beautiful experience. This takes time. In our hurried world we don't always have the time. That is the reality of the world that we live in. It is what it is. But the real lesson here is that it is worth the wait. None of this will happen overnight. We will step on each other's toes, forget the steps, get upset and slide backwards at times. But our mistakes and miscues can be short-lived if we keep trying. If we don't give up and keep returning to the dance floor we will make progress. And the next time we meet we are in a better place.

Adolescents don't forget. They know the time and love we put forth—they also know when we pull power trips. They may not admit right away or all the time -- but they know. They also know that they are not getting the same love or attention in other areas of their life and they come around. Each step brings us closer to relating better, enjoying each other more, understanding each other and ultimately allowing us to enjoy a beautiful and fulfilling dance. Enjoy.

Author Bios

The author with his wife, Karyn, and their dogs, Dizzy and Charlie.

Jeff Beedy is a pioneer and leader in sport-based education. Jeff's original doctoral thesis in the early 1980's charted the cartography of a new domain — sports as moral pedagogy, built on a foundation of research and experience.

At Harvard, Jeff studied with renowned child psychologists Carol Gilligan, Lawrence Kohlberg, Robert Selman, and Sesame Street founder Gerald Lesser. Jeff taught Social Reflections of Literature for Pulitzer Prize-winner Dr. Robert Coles.

Jeff's previous work, PLUS: Positive Learning Using Sports, is used around the globe, including China, South Korea, and throughout the United States and Canada. Jeff's PLUS model for child development was used in conjunction with a United Nation's grant and the Olympic Doves Movement to bridge peace between the Greek and Turkish children on the island of Cyprus.

In 2010, Jeff became the founding head of Korea International School, which was the first boarding school to open in South Korea's $2 billion Global Education City on Jeju Island.

Jeff is currently, working on a new book entitled, *The Other Classroom: Reframing Children's Sports to Teach Survival Skills.*

In his earlier years, Jeff played in the Cape Cod Baseball league and skied in the freestyle tour. Jeff and his wife Karyn are musicians and play professionally as the Nadia and Jocko Band.

***

Matt Cheney worked for ten years as a high school teacher at schools in New Hampshire and New Jersey before pursuing a PhD in Literature at the University of New Hampshire. He won the Hudson Prize for his debut fiction collection BLOOD: STORIES (Black Lawrence Press, 2016).

www.ingramcontent.com/pod-product-compliance
Lightning Source LLC
Chambersburg PA
CBHW051833040426
42447CB00006B/501
9780985522315